AF375224

Python Programming

An In-Depth Approach

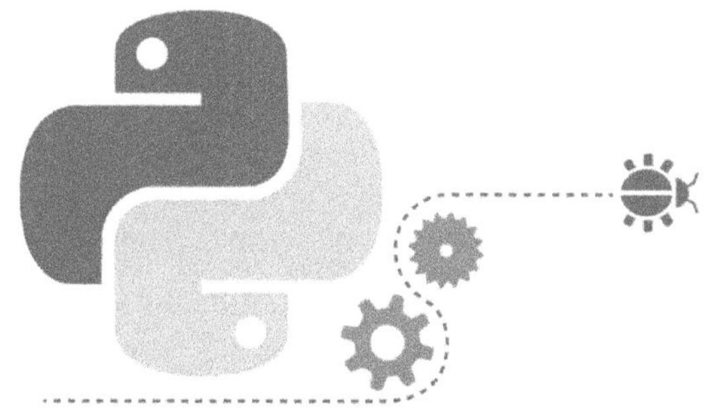

Prof. Kalyani N. Satone

Dr. Anushree Deshmukh

Prof. Ankush Hutke

Dr. Sunil Wankhade

This book has been published with utmost care to ensure error-free content, following the author's consent. However, the author and publisher disclaim any liability for loss, damage, or disruption caused by errors or omissions, whether due to negligence, accident, or other causes.

Despite all efforts to avoid mistakes or omissions, this publication is sold with the understanding that neither the author, publishers, nor printers shall be held liable for any errors, omissions, or any actions taken (or omitted) based on the content of this work. In the case of printing or binding defects, the publisher's liability is limited to replacing the defective copy with another, subject to availability.

Copyright © <2025 > < Prof. Kalyani N. Satone,Dr. Anushree Deshmukh,Prof. Ankush Hutke,Dr. Sunil Wankhade>

❋ *Dedicates to...*

I dedicate this book to my husband Nakul, my parents, my sons Harsh and Yash, and my in-laws. Their unwavering support made this book possible. May this work reflect the limitless potential that comes from dedication and the support of family.

I am deeply grateful for your presence in my life; it is the greatest gift I could ever receive.

Kalyani Satone

I am deeply grateful to Almighty and my family for their constant support.

- *Anushree Deshmukh*
  Ankush Hutke
  Sunil Wankhade

Preface

Welcome to the world of Python, a programming language that has revolutionized the way we think about software development. Python's simplicity and versatility make it an excellent choice for both beginners and experienced programmers. This book is designed to guide you through the fundamental concepts and advanced features of Python.

Python's clean syntax and readability have made it a popular language for a variety of applications, ranging from web development to data science, from automation scripts to complex machine learning algorithms.

In this book, we will embark on a journey through Python's capabilities. We will start with the basics, exploring variables, data types, and control structures. As we progress, we will delve into more complex topics such as object-oriented programming, file handling, and error management.

We are excited to share the beauty and power of Python with you. This book is more than just a guide; it is an invitation to join a vibrant and dynamic community of developers who are shaping the future of technology. Together, let's unlock the potential of Python and open the door to endless possibilities.

Happy coding!

Authors

Prof. Kalyani N. Satone

Dr. Anushree Deshmukh

Prof. Ankush Hutke

Dr. Sunil Wankhade

About the Author

Prof.Kalyani Satone, an Assistant Professor at St. Vincent Pallotti College of Engineering and Technology, Nagpur, brings 19 years of experience in Computer Science and Engineering. Currently pursuing her Ph.D., She is a prolific author with four internationally published books, including Java Programming, Excel for Managers, and Object-Oriented Modelling and Design. Her expertise and research have been recognized at national and international conferences.

Dr. Anushree Deshmukh, an Assistant Professor at MCT's Rajiv Gandhi Institute of Technology, Mumbai, brings over 15 years of academic expertise to her work. With a Ph.D. in Science and Technology and a deep passion for Python programming, she has crafted a resourceful guide that bridges technical proficiency and real-world application for learners of all levels.

Prof. Ankush Hutke, Assistant Professor at MCT's Rajiv Gandhi Institute of Technology, Mumbai, has over 19 years of experience as an educator. With a background in Computer Science and Information Technology, he has authored and reviewed numerous research papers in journals and international conferences. His expertise spans computer programming, algorithms, machine learning, and big data analytics.

Dr. Sunil Wankhade, Professor and Head of the Information Technology Department at MCT's Rajiv Gandhi Institute of Technology, Mumbai, brings 32 years of expertise to his teaching. Specializing in Python programming, Machine Learning, and Wireless Technologies, he has guided learners from beginners to advanced developers. Through research, mentoring, and workshops, he has empowered professionals across industries to excel in data science, web development, and automation.

Contents

Contents

1.

Introduction to Python Programming

Unit Structure:

1.0 Python Interpreter and Interactive Mode

Introduction

The name Python was selected from the TV Show "The Complete Monty Python's Circus", which was broadcasted in BBC from 1969 to 1974. Guido developed Python language by taking almost all programming features from different languages

1. Functional Programming Features from C
2. Object Oriented Programming Features from C++
3. Scripting Language Features from Perl and Shell Script
4. Modular Programming Features from Modula-3

Where we can use Python:

We can use it everywhere. The most common important application areas are :

1. For developing Desktop Applications
2. For developing web Applications
3. For developing database Applications
4. For Network Programming
6. For Data Analysis Applications
7. For developing Artificial Intelligence Applications

Internally Google and Youtube use Python coding. NASA and Network Stock Exchange Applications developed by Python. Top Software companies like Google, Microsoft, IBM, Yahoo using Python.

Features of Python:

1. Simple and easy to learn

2. Freeware and Open Source

3. High Level Programming language

4. Platform Independent

5. Portability

6. Dynamically Typed

7. Both Procedure Oriented and Object Oriented

8. Extensive Library

Python Mode: Python has two basic modes: script and interactive.

1. Interactive mode:

Interactive mode is based on working simultaneously. In the interactive mode as we enter a command and press enter, the very next step we get the output. The output of the code in the interactive mode is influenced by the last command we give. Interactive mode is very convenient for writing very short lines of code.

How to run python code in Interactive mode?

To run our program in an interactive mode, we can use command prompt in windows, terminal in Linux, and macOS.

Example 1:

To run python in command prompt type "python". Then simply type the Python statement on >>> prompt. As we type and press enter we can see the output in the very next line.

Python program to display "Hello Students"

print("Hello Students")

print("This is our first session")

Output:

```
IDLE Shell 3.11.3
File  Edit  Shell  Debug  Options  Window  Help
    Python 3.11.3 (tags/v3.11.3:f3909b8, Apr  4 2023, 23:49:59) [MSC v.1934 64 bit (AMD64)] on win32
    Type "help", "copyright", "credits" or "license()" for more information.
>>> print("hello students")
    hello students
>>> print("This is our first session")
    This is our first session
>>>
```

>>> a=2

>>> b=3

>>> c=a+b

>>> print(c)

Note:

>>> print("c")

c

If we write in double quotations then alphabet will be printed only as it is treated as a character.

Example:

a=2

print(a*7)

Output:14

>>> s= "hello"*4

>>> print(s)

hellohellohellohello

>>>output: 'hellohellohellohello'

Print(type(a))

Output is: int

Disadvantages of Interactive Mode:

The interactive mode is not suitable for large programs.

The interactive mode doesn't save the statements. Once we make a program it is for that time itself, we cannot use it in the future. In order to use it in the future, we need to retype all the statements.

2. **Script Mode:**

In the script mode, a python program can be written in a file. This file can then be saved and executed using the command prompt. We can view the code at any time by opening the file and editing becomes quite easy as we can open and view the entire code as many times as we want.

Script mode is very suitable for writing long pieces of code. It is much preferred over interactive mode by experts in the program. The file made in the script mode is by default saved in the Python installation folder and the extension to save a python file is ".py".

How to run python code in script mode?

To run a code in script mode follow the following steps.

Step 1: Make a file using a text editor. You can use any text editor of your choice.

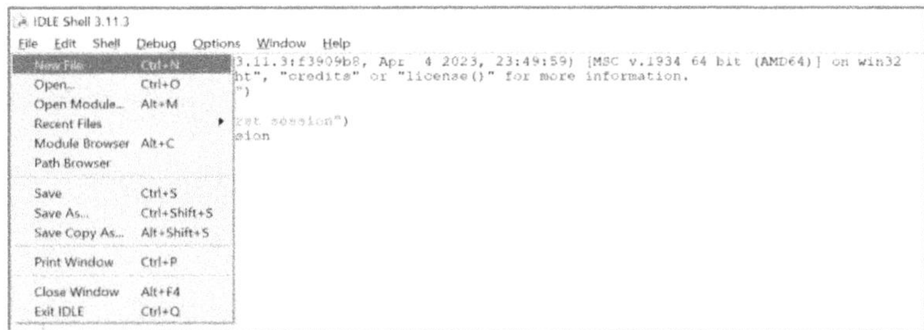

Step 2: After writing the code save the file using ".py" extension.

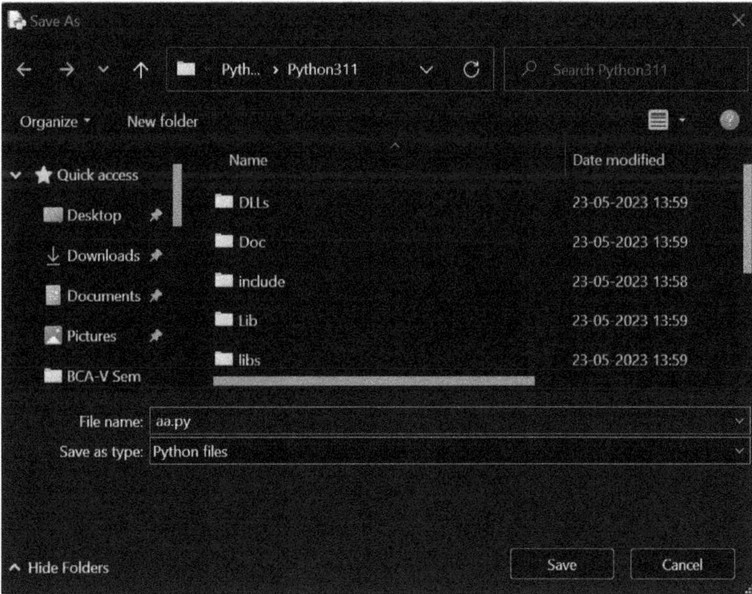

Step 3: Now run the file.

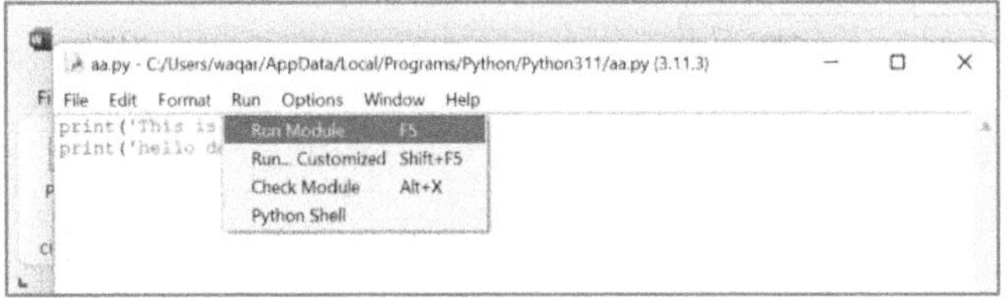

1.1 Variables and Identifiers.

Python variable is also known as an identifier and used to hold value.

Rules for declaring an identifier

1. The equal (=) operator is used to assign value to a variable. The only allowed characters in Python are alphabets (either lower case or upper case), digits (0 to 9) and underscore symbol (_).

   cash = 10 ➔ valid

   ca$h =20 ➔ error

2. Identifier should not start with digit.

   a1=5 # Valid

   1a=5 # Error

3. Identifiers are case sensitive. Of course Python language is case sensitive language.

total=10

TOTAL=999

print(total)

print(TOTAL)

4. No reserve word can be used as an identifier

e.g.

if=100 ➔ Error

fi=100 ➔ valid

for=7 ➔Error

Reserved Words (Keywords)

Keywords are words with special meaning in language.

There are 35 reserve words in Python.

False	None	True	and	as	assert	async
await	break	class	continue	def	del	elif
else	except	finally	for	from	global	If
import	in	Is	lambda	nonlocal	not	or
pass	raise	return	try	while	with	yield

Note:

1. All Reserved words in Python contain only the alphabet.

2. Except the first 3 reserved words, all others contain only lower case alphabets. True, False, None

input()

input() function can be used to read data directly from keyboard. It reads the value in the form of string only.

Program

```
x=input("Your name please?  :")
print("Hello ",x, " Good Morning")
```

Output

```
Your name please?  :Ajay
Hello  Ajay  Good Morning
```

To perform arithmetic operations on numbers, the text(string) values are to be converted into equivalent numbers using conversion functions like int() or float()

Program to read 2 numbers from the keyboard and print sum.

Expected Output

```
Enter First Number:100
Enter Second Number:200

The Sum: 300
```

Program:

```
x=int(input("Enter First Number:"))
y=int(input("Enter Second Number:"))
print("The Sum:",x+y)
```

Output statements:

print() function :This function is used to display output.

Format 1:

print() without any argument

It just prints new line character

```
print("Good Morning")
print()
print("Good Evening")
```

output

```
Good Morning

Good Evening
```

Format 2:

Using Escape characters "\n" and "\t"

```
print("Hello World")
print("Hello \n World")
print("Hello \t World")
```

Output

```
Hello World
Hello
World
Hello   World
```

Format 3:

Using "Sep" attribute

By default output values are seperated by space. If we want we can specify seperator by using "sep" attribute

Program:

```
a,b,c=10,20,30

print(a,b,c,sep=",")
print(a,b,c,sep=";")
```

Output

```
10,20,30
10:20:30
```

1.2 Operators.

Operator is a symbol that performs certain operations. Data on which operator operates is called as operand. Combination of operator and operand is called as Expression.

a+ b -5

Python provides the following set of operators

1.Arithmetic Operators

2. Relational Operators or Comparison Operators

3. Logical operators

4. Assignment operators

5. Special operators

Arithmetic Operators

Arithmetic operators can perform common mathematical operations

+	Add
-	Subtract
*	Multiply
/	Float Divide
%	Mod [Remainder]

| // | Integer Division |
| ** | Power or Exponent |

Program

```
a=10
b=2

print('a+b=',a+b)
print('a-b=',a-b)
print('a*b=',a*b)

print('a%b=',a%b)
print('b%a=',b%a)

print('a**b=',a**b)
print('b**a=',b**a)

a=27
b=10
print('a/b=',a/b)
print('a//b=',a//b)
```

Output:

```
a+b= 12
a-b= 8
a*b= 20
a%b= 0
b%a= 2
a**b= 100
b**a= 1024
a/b= 2.7
a//b= 2
```

Logical Operators

The assessment of expressions to make decisions typically makes use of the logical operators. The following logical operators are supported by Python.

Operator	Description
And	The condition will also be true if the expression is true. If the two expressions a and b are the same, then a and b must both be true.
Or	The condition will be true if one of the phrases is true. If a and b are the two expressions, then an or b must be true if and is true and b is false.
Not	If an expression a is true, then not (a) will be false and vice versa.

Relational /Comparison operator

Comparison operators compare the values of the two operands and return a true or false Boolean value in accordance. The following table lists the comparison operators.

Operator	Description
==	If the value of two operands is equal, then the condition becomes true.
!=	If the value of two operands is not equal, then the condition becomes true.
<=	The condition is met if the first operand is smaller than or equal to the second operand.
>=	The condition is met if the first operand is greater than or equal to the second operand.
>	If the first operand is greater than the second operand, then the condition becomes true.
<	If the first operand is less than the second operand, then the condition becomes true.

Assignment Operators

The right expression's value is assigned to the left operand using the assignment operators. The following table provides a description of the assignment operators.

Operator	Description
=	It assigns the value of the right expression to the left operand.
+=	By multiplying the value of the right operand by the value of the left operand, the left operand receives a changed value. For example, if a = 10, b = 20 => a+ = b will be equal to a = a+ b and therefore, a = 30.
-=	It decreases the value of the left operand by the value of the right operand and assigns the modified value back to left operand. For example, if a = 20, b = 10 => a- = b will be equal to a = a- b and therefore, a = 10.
*=	It multiplies the value of the left operand by the value of the right operand and assigns the modified value back to then the left operand. For example, if a = 10, b = 20 => a* = b will be equal to a = a* b and therefore, a = 200.
%=	It divides the value of the left operand by the value of the right operand and assigns the reminder back to the left operand. For example, if a = 20, b = 10 => a % = b will be equal to a = a % b and therefore, a = 0.
**=	a**=b will be equal to a=a**b, for example, if a = 4, b =2, a**=b will assign 4**2 = 16 to a.
//=	A//=b will be equal to a = a// b, for example, if a = 4, b = 3, a//=b will assign 4//3 = 1 to a.

id() function :

The id() function, is used to identify the object identifier.
Consider the following example.

```
a = 25
b = a
print(id(a))
print(id(b))
# Reassigned variable a
a = 500
print(id(a))
```

output

```
2594254187568
2594254187568
2594260286064
```

Multiple Assignment:

```
x=y=z=25

print(x)

print(y)

print(z)
```

Output:

```
25

25

25
```

Assigning multiple values to multiple variables:

```
a, b, c=10, 20, 30
print a
print b
print c
```

Output:

```
10
20
30
```

1.3 Data Types.

Integer (int)

We can use int data type to represent whole numbers without decimal points (integral values). Integers in Python are of unlimited size.

```
a=10
print(type(a))
```

output

```
(int)
```

float

We can use float data type to represent floating point values (decimal values)

Eg:

```
f=1.234
print( type(f) )
```

output

```
(float)
```

We can also represent floating point values by using exponential form (scientific notation)

program:

```
x=1.25e3
y=5750e-3
print(x)
print(y)
```

output

```
    1250.0
    5.75
```

Complex

A complex number is of the form. a and b contain integers or floating point values

e.g.

3+5j   10+5.5j   0.5+0.1j

Program:

```
a=10+1.5j
b=20+2.5j

c=a+b

print(c)
print(type(c))
```

output

```
(30+4j)
```

```
<class 'complex'>
```

We can use complex type generally in scientific Applications.

boolean

We can use this data type to represent Boolean values. The only allowed values for this data type are: True and False

```
x=5<7

y=5>7

print(x,y)

print(type(x))
```

output

```
True False
<class 'bool'>
```

String

A String is a sequence of characters enclosed within single quotes or double quotes.

s1='India'

s1="India"

Program:

```
x="Wardha"
print(x)
print(type(x))
```

Output

```
Wardha
<class 'Str'>
```

List

List is a collection of data items enclosed in square brackets.

Program

```
x=[100,45.3, "hello",True]

print(x)
```

Output

```
=[100,45.3, "hello",True]
```

List may contain homogenous or heterogeneous items

Program

```
x=[10,20,30,40,50]
y=["india","Australia","America"]
z=[10,"India","America",30]
print(x)
print(y)
print(z)
```

Output

```
[10,20,30,40,50]
["india","Australia","America"]
[10,"India","America",30]
```

Using for loop to access List items

Loop is a block of statements which is repeatedly executed. For loop will be executed as many times as the number of items in the List.

Program

```
x=[10,"India",2.25,True]
y=[500,600,700]

for i in x:
    print(i)

print("----------")

for i in y:
    print(i)
```

Output

```
10
India
2.25
True
500
600
700
```

Characteristics of List Data Type

1.   List values enclosed in square brackets [ ]

2.   List allows duplicate items

3.   Index is used to access individual items

4.   Insertion order is preserved

5.   List items can be edited or modified

6.   List is growable i.e. items can be added or removed from the List

Tuple

Tuple data type is exactly same as list data type except that it is immutable .i.e. we cannot edit or modify the Tuple items. Tuple values are enclosed in parenthesis ( ).

Program:

```
t=(10,20,30,40)
print(t)
```

Output:

```
(10,20,30,40)
```

Program

```
t=(10,20,3.25,"India")
print(t[0])
print(t[1])
print(t[2])
print(t[3])
```

Output

```
10
20
3.25
India
```

Tuple is Read Only

If an attempt is made to edit or modify the tuple data, it results in error.

```
t=(10,20,3.25,"India")
print("Before")
print(t)
t[0]=125
print("After")
print(t)
```

Output

```
Error
```

Characteristics of Tuple Data Type

1   Tuple values enclosed in parenthesis ()

2   Tuple allows duplicate items

3   Index is used to access individual Tuple items

4   Insertion order is preserved

5   Tuple items cannot be edited or modified

6   Tuple is not grow able i.e. items cannot be added or removed from Tuple

Range

Range Data Type represents a sequence of numbers.

Program

```
x=range(5)

print(x)
```

Output

```
range(0, 5)
```

Using for loop to access range values

Specifying upper and lower limit

Program

```
x=range(10,15)
for i in x:
    print(i)
```

Output

```
10
11
12
```

```
13
14
```

1.4 Type Conversions

There are two types of type conversion in Python.

- Implicit Conversion - automatic type conversion

- Explicit Conversion - manual type conversion

Python Implicit Type Conversion

In certain situations, Python automatically converts one data type to another. This is known as implicit type conversion.

Example 1: Converting integer to float

Conversion of the lower data type (integer) to the higher data type (float) to avoid data loss.

```
I= 123
F = 1.23

Res=I+F

print("Value:",Res)
print("Data Type:",type(Res))
```

Output

```
Value: 124.23

Data Type: <class 'float'>
```

As we can see Res has value 124.23 and is of the float data type.

It is because Python always converts smaller data types to larger data types to avoid the loss of data.

Note:

- We get TypeError, if we try to add str and int. For example, '12' + 23. Python is not able to use Implicit Conversion in such conditions.

- Python has a solution for these types of situations which is known as Explicit Conversion.

Explicit Type Conversion

In Explicit Type Conversion, users convert the data type of an object to required data type.

We use the built-in functions like int(), float(), str(), etc to perform explicit type conversion.

This type of conversion is also called typecasting because the user casts (changes) the data type of the objects.

```
a=10
b="20"
print(type(a))
print(type(b))
b=int(b)
print(type(b))
c=a+b
print(c)
print(type(c))
```

Output

```
<class 'int'>
<class 'str'>
<class 'int'>
30
<class 'int'>
```

1.5 Control statements.

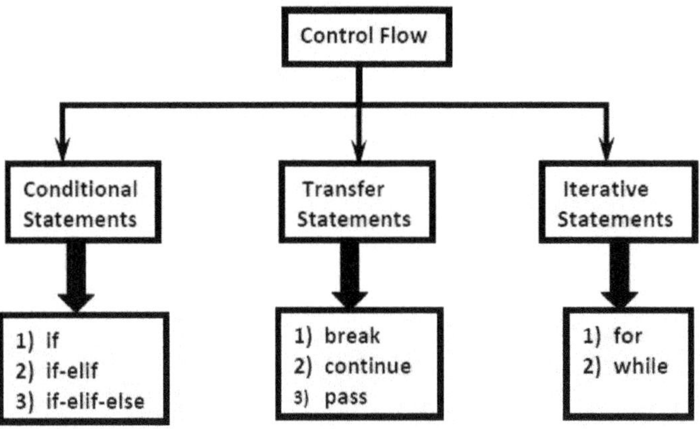

Conditional Statements

If statement

It consists of keyword if followed by condition. If the result of condition is true then statements in the block are executed. If block may contain either one or multiple statements.

If condition: statement

Or

If condition:
Statement-1
Statement-2
Statement-3
If condition is true then statements will be executed

Expected Output

Enter a number:150
Number greater than 100

Program

```
n=int(input("Enter a number:")
if n>100: print("Number greater than 100")
```

Or

```
n=int(input("Enter a number:")
if n>100:
        print("Number greater than 100")
```

```
Enter a number:50
```

If-else statement

The if block may be followed by else block. When the condition in if is false, then the statement in the else block are executed. Else is never followed by condition.

```
if condition :

        Statement-1
        Statement-2
else :

        Statement-3
        Statement-2
```

Program to check whether the given number is in between 50 and 100

```
n=int(input("Enter Number:"))

if n>=50 and n<=100 :
        print("The number",n,"is in between 50 to 100")
else:
        print("The number",n,"is not in between 50 to 100")
```

Output

```
Enter Number:150
The number 150 is not in between 50 to 100
```

if-elif-else statement

The if statement may be followed by one or more elif statements where different conditions are specified. Statements in the elif block where the condition is true gets executed. If the condition in if and all the elif blocks is false, then the statements in else block are executed.

Syntax:

```
if condition1:
        statements
elif condition2:
        statements
elif condition3:
        statements
elif condition4:
        statements
else:
        statements
```

Program to check whether the entered number is greater than, less than or equal to 100.

Expected Output

```
Enter a number
50
Less than 100
```

Program:

```
n=int(input("Enter a number") )

if n>100 :
    print("Greater than 100")
elif n<100:
    print("Less than 100")
else :
    print("Equal to 100")
```

1.6 Loop Structures

If we want to execute a group of statements multiple times then we should go for Iterative statements. Python supports 2 types of iterative statements.

1. for loop
2. while loop

for loop

If we want to execute some action for every element present in some sequence then we should go for for loop.

Syntax:

```
for variable_name in sequence :
        statements
```

where sequence can be string or any collection. Body will be executed for every element present in the sequence.

To print Hello 10 times
```
for x in range(10) :
    print("Hello")
```

While loop

If we want to execute a group of statements iteratively until some condition false, then we should go for while loop.

Syntax:

```
while condition :
    statements
```

To print numbers from 1 to 5 by using while loop

```
x=1

while x <=5:
    print(x)
    x=x+1
```

Output

1

2

3

4

5

Nested Loops

A loop may be defined inside another loop, which are also known as nested loops.

Program

```
for i in range(3):
    for j in range(2):
        print("i=",i," j=",j)
    print("------------")
```

Output

```
i= 0  j= 0
i= 0  j= 1
------------
i= 1  j= 0
i= 1  j= 1
------------
i= 2  j= 0
i= 2  j= 1
------------
```

Program to display "*" is right angled triangle form as shown

Expected Output

```
*
* *
* * *
* * * *
* * * * *
```

Program

```
for i in range(1,6):
    for j in range(1,i+1):
        print("*",end=" ")
    print()
```

1.7 Transfer Statements

break

The break statement is used to terminate the execution of the loop in between. When break statement executed, the loop is terminated and control is transferred out of the loop.

Program

```
for i in range(10):
    print("Hello")

    if i==2:
        break

print("Good Day")
```

Output
  Hello
  Hello
  Hello
  Good Day

Continue

Continue statement is used to transfer the control to the beginning of the loop. When continue statement is executed, the control will jump to the loop beginning.

Program

```
for i in range(10):
    if i%2==0:
        continue
    print(i)
```

Output

```
1
3
5
7
9
```

Pass statement:

In Python, the pass statement is a null operation. When it's executed, nothing happens. It is used as a placeholder in situations where some code is syntactically required but you haven't written the actual code yet. This can be useful in loops, function definitions, or conditional statements where you plan to add code later.

```
x = 10

if x > 0:

    pass

else:

    print ("x is not positive")
```

The pass statement ensures that the code runs without errors even if the implementation is incomplete.

1.8 Summary

Python's interpreter and interactive mode enable developers to execute code line-by-line, making it ideal for testing and learning. Variables in Python are containers for storing data, each identified by a name (identifier) adhering to specific rules. Python supports standard arithmetic operators such as addition, subtraction, multiplication, division, modulus, and more, facilitating numerical computations.

Values in Python can be integers, floats, strings, or other data types, each with its own characteristics and uses. Statements control the flow of execution, including conditional statements (if, if...else, if...elif...else), loops (while, for), and flow control (continue, break). Python's dynamic and strongly-typed nature allows flexible and secure handling of data types during runtime, supporting efficient and clear programming practices.

1.9 Questions

Multiple Choice Questions

1.What is the purpose of the Python interpreter?

A) To convert Python code into machine code
B) To execute Python code line-by-line interactively
C) To compile Python code into an executable file
D) To debug Python programs

2. Which of the following is a valid Python identifier?

A) 2variable   B) _myVar   C) my Variable   D) if

3. What does the type() function in Python do?

A) Converts a variable to a different type   B) Checks if two variables refer to the same object
C) Returns the type of an object   D) Converts a string to uppercase

4.Which operator is used for exponentiation in Python?
A) **   B) //   C) %   D) ^

5.What statement is used to terminate a for loop prematurely in Python?

A) halt   B) stop   C) end   D) break

Long Answer Questions

1. Explain the concept of variables and identifiers in Python.
2. Describe operators in Python. Provide examples of each operator.
3. Discuss the various data types available in Python and their characteristics.
4. Explain the importance of control flow statements in Python programming.
5. Discuss the Loop structures in Python.

2.

Functions

Unit Structure:

2.0   Functions

Functions:

If a group of statements is repeatedly executed, then it is not recommended to write these statements every time separately. We have to define these statements as a single unit, and we can call that unit any number of times based on our requirement without rewriting. This unit is nothing but function.

The main advantage of functions is code Reusability.

Note: In other languages functions are known as methods, procedures, subroutines etc.

Python supports 2 types of functions

1. Built in Functions
2. User Defined Functions

1. Built in Functions:

The functions which are coming along with Python software automatically are called built-in functions or pre-defined functions.

e.g.: id(), type(), input(),print() etc..

2. User Defined Functions:

The functions which are developed by programmer explicitly according to business requirements are called user defined functions.

Syntax to create user defined functions:

```
def function_name(parameters) :
    ----
    statements
    ----
```

Example:

```
def abc():
    print("good morning")

print("hello")
abc()
print("good day")
abc()
```

Output

```
hello
good morning
good day
good morning
```

Function arguments or parameters

Values can be passed to the function in the form of arguments or parameters. The function arguments or parameters are specified in the pair parenthesis following the function name.

The value for function arguments are passed while calling the function. A function can accept any number of arguments which may be of any data type.

Function to add two numbers

```
def abc(x,y):
    z=x+y
    print("sum=",z)


a,b=10,20
abc(a,b)
abc(5,7)
abc(10,50)
```

Output

```
sum= 30
sum= 12
sum= 60
```

Program to find factorial of numbers from 1 to 5

```
def fact(num):
    result=1

    while num>=1:
        result=result*num
        num=num-1
    return result


for i in range(1,6):
print(i," != ",fact(i))
```

Output

```
1 != 1
2 != 2
3 != 6
4 != 24
5 != 120
```

Return Statement

Function can take input values as parameters and returns output to the caller with return statement.

Function to accept two numbers as input and return sum.

```python
def add(x,y):
    return x+y

result=add(10,20)

print("The sum is",result)
print("The sum is",add(100,200))
```

Output

```
The sum is 30
The sum is 300
```

Returning multiple values from a function

In other languages like C,C++ and Java, function can return at most one value. But in Python, a function can return any number of values.

Eg:

```
def sum_sub(a,b):
sum=a+b
sub=a-b
return sum,sub
```

```
x,y=sum_sub(100,50)

print("The Sum is :",x)
print("The Subtraction is :",y)
```

Output

```
The Sum is : 150
The Subtraction is : 50
```

Recursive Functions

A function that calls itself is known as Recursive Function.

Eg:

factorial(3)=3*factorial(2)

=3*2*factorial(1)

=3*2*1*factorial(0)

=3*2*1*1

=6

factorial(n)= n*factorial(n-1)

The main advantages of recursive functions are:

1. We can reduce length of the code and improves readability

2. We can solve complex problems very easily.

Function to find factorial of given number with recursion.

Example:

```
def factorial(n):
    if n==0:
        result=1
    else:
        result=n*factorial(n-1)
    return result


print("Factorial of 4 is :",factorial(4))
```

Output

```
Factorial of 4 is : 24
```

2.1 Types of Arguments

Types of arguments

```
def f1(a,b):
        ------
        ------
        ------


f1(10,20)
```

a,b are formal arguments whereas 10,20 are actual arguments

There are 4 types are actual arguments are allowed in Python.

1. positional arguments

2. keyword arguments

3. default arguments

4. Variable length arguments

1. Positional arguments:

These are the arguments passed to function in correct positional order.

```
def sub(a,b):
        print(a-b)


sub(100,200)
sub(200,100)
```

The number of arguments and position of arguments must be matched. If we change the order, then result may be changed. If we change the number of arguments, then we will get error.

2. Keyword arguments:

We can pass argument values by keyword i.e by parameter name.
Example:

```
def xyz(x,y):
    print("Hello",x,y)


xyz(x="Sanjay",y="Good Morning")
xyz(y="Good Morning",x="Ajay")
```

Output

```
Hello Sanjay Good Morning
Hello Ajay Good Morning
```

Here the order of arguments is not important, but number of arguments must be matched.

3. Default Arguments:

Sometimes we can provide default values for our positional arguments.
Example:

```
def xyz(x="Ajit"):
    print("Hello",x,"Good Morning")


xyz("Sanjay")
xyz()
```

Output

Hello Sanjay Good Morning

Hello Ajit Good Morning

4. Variable length arguments:

Variable-length arguments, abbreviated as varargs, are defined as arguments that can also accept an unlimited amount of data as input. The developer doesn't have to wrap the data in a list or any other sequence while using them.

There are two types of variable-length arguments in Python-

Non - Keyworded Arguments denoted as (*args)
Keyworded Arguments denoted as (**kwargs)

Non - Keyworded Arguments (args)

To provide variable-length parameters, we need to use an asterisk before the parameter name in the given method. The type of parameters supplied is a tuple, and within the method, these passed arguments form a tuple with the same name as the parameter, excluding the asterisk.

Features of args
*args defines the number of non-keyworded arguments, and we can perform the operations on the tuple. It makes the function flexible.

Example: Using * args to pass the variable-length arguments to the function and finding the multiplication.

Sometimes we can pass variable number of arguments to our function, such type of arguments are called variable length arguments.

We can declare a variable length argument with * symbol as follows

$$def\ f1(*n):$$

We can call this function by passing any number of arguments including zero number.

Internally all these values represented in the form of tuple.

Example:

```
def xyz(*n):
   t=0
   for i in n:
     t=t+i
   print("The Sum=",t)


xyz()
xyz (10)
xyz (10,20)
xyz (10,20,30,40)
```

Output

```
The Sum= 0
The Sum= 10
The Sum= 30
The Sum= 100
```

Keyworded Arguments (kwargs)

Python uses args to provide a variable-length non-keyword argument to a function, but it cannot be used to pass a keyword argument. kwargs, a Python solution for this problem, is used to pass the variable length of keyword arguments to the method.

To indicate such an argument, we need to use a double asterisk before the parameter's name in the method. Arguments are supplied in the dictionary, which creates a dictionary within the method with a name similar to the parameter except for double asterisk **

Features of kwargs

**kwargs is responsible for passing a variable number of keyword arguments dictionary to the method, allowing it to perform dictionary operations.

It is known as kwargs because of the double star. The double star allows us to send keyword arguments through (and any number of them). When you pass a variable into a function as a keyword argument, you give it a name.

The kwargs can be thought of as a dictionary that maps each term to the value we pass along with it, which is why there doesn't appear to be any sequence in which the kwargs were printed out when we iterate over them.

Example:

```
def abcd(**arg):
        for key, value in arg.items():
                print (key, ":" , value)
abcd(a="hello",b="fine",c="namaste")
```

Output:

```
a : hello
b : fine
c : namaste
```

Using args and kwargs to Call a Function

We can also use *args and **kwargs to pass arguments into functions.

```python
def xyz(a,b,c):

    print("Argument 1:", a)

    print("Argument 2:", b)

    print("Argument 3:", c)



# printing values

args = ("Mumbai", "Nagpur", "Wardha")

xyz(*args)
```

output

```
Argument 1: Mumbai

Argument 2: Nagpur

Argument 3: Wardha
```

2.2 Scope and Lifetime of Variables.

Types of Variables

Python supports two types of variables.

1. Global Variables

2. Local Variables

Global Variables

The variables which are declared outside of function are called global variables. These variables can be accessed in all functions of that module.

Local Variables

The variables which are declared inside the function are called local variables. These variables can be accessed within the function only.

Example:

```
a=10        # global variable
def f1():
    b=20    #local variable
    print(a)


def f2():
    print(a)


f1()
f2()
```

Output

```
10
20
10
```

2.3 Commonly used modules.

Module is a group of variables and functions saved in a file.

There are two types of modules in Python,

1.   Pre Defined Modules
2.   User Defined Modules

Modules which are already defined or present in the language are called as predefined modules.

- Predefined modules contain predefined functions.

- Modules created by the user are called as user defined modules. User defined modules contain user defined functions.

Predefined Modules In Python

Math Module

A Module is collection of functions and variables and constants. Math is a module that contains several functions to perform mathematical operations. If we want to use any module in Python, first we have to import that module.

import math
Once we import a module then we can call any function of that module.

Program:

```
import math

print(math.pi)
print(math.sqrt(25))
```

Output:

```
3.141592653589793
5.0
```

Creating A Module Alias

An alias means alternate name. We can create alias name by using 'as' keyword.

import math as m

Now 'm' is an alias or alternate name for 'math' module.

Once we create alias name, by using that we can access functions and variables of that module

```
import math as m


print(m.pi)
print(m.sqrt(25))
```

Output

```
3.141592653589793
5.0
```

Importing All members of module

To import all members of a module '*' symbol is used.

e.g.

from math import *

Important functions of math module:

1.   sqrt(x)

2.   sin(x)

3.   cos(x)

4.   tan(x)

5.   pow(x,y)

6.   factorial(x)

Program:

```
from math import *
print(pow(5,3))
print(sqrt(4))
print(ceil(10.1))
print(floor(10.1))
print(factorial(5))
```

Output:

```
125.0
2.0
11
10
120
```

Random Module

This module defines several functions to generate random numbers. Random numbers can be used in applications like OTP generation.

random () function

This function always generates some float value between 0 and 1 (not inclusive) $0<x<1$

Program:

```
from random import *

print (random ())
print (random ())
print (random ())
```

Output

```
0.4572685609302056
0.6584325233197768
0.15444034016553587
```

randint() function

To generate random integer between two given numbers (both inclusive)

```python
from random import *

print(randint(1,100))
print(randint(1,100))
print(randint(1,100))
```

Output:

```
13
95
63
```

choice() function

It will return a random object from the given list or tuple.

```python
from random import *

x=["Wardha","Nagpur","Mumbai","Chennai","Pune"]

for i in range(3):
    print(choice(x))
```

Output:

Pune

Mumbai

Chennai

Creating User Defined Modules

1.Crete a new Python File "abc123.py"

2.Write following functions in the file "abc123.py"

Program In File abc123.py

```python
def show():
        print("Function show is executed")
def display():
        print("Function display is executed")
```

Importing A Module

To execute functions in a module, the module is to be imported.

'import' statement is used to import a module to the program.

1.   Create a new file 'xyz.py'

2.   Import module 'abc' in the file

3.   Call show() and display() functions present in the module 'abc'

Program in File xyz.py

```
import abc123

abc123.show()
abc123.display()
```

Output:

```
Function show is executed
Function display is executed
```

Create a new module in the file demo1.py containing two functions sum() and product()

Program in file demo1.py

```
def sum(a,b):
        print("Sum=",a+b)

def product(a,b):
        print("Product=",a*b)
```

Import module demo1.py in the file demo2.py and call the sum() and product functions to find the sum and product of numbers 10 and 20.

Program in file demo2.py

```
import demo1
demo1.sum(10,20)
demo1.product(10,20)
```

Output:

Sum=30

Product=200

2.4   Command Line Arguments.

The Arguments which are passing at the time of execution are called Command Line Arguments.

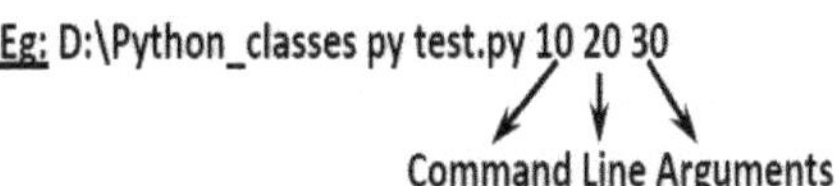

Within the Python Program this Command Line Arguments are available in argv. Which is present in SYS Module.

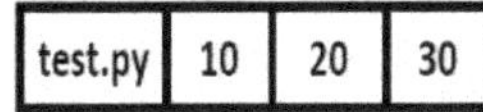

Note: argv[0] represents Name of Program. But not first Command Line Argument.

argv[1] represent First Command Line Argument.

```
from sys import argv

print('The Number of Command Line Arguments:", len(argv))
print("The List of Command Line Arguments:", argv)
print("Command Line Arguments one by one:")

for x in argv:
        print(x)
```

Output

```
C:\Users\abc>demo.py 10 20 30
The Number of Command Line Arguments: 4

The List of Command Line Arguments: ['demo.py', '10', '20', '30']
Command Line Arguments one by one:
demo.py
10
20
30
```

Program to accept radius as a command line argument and find the area of the circle
from sys import argv

```
from math import pi,pow

r=float(argv[1])
a=pi*pow(r,2)

print("The area of circle is:",a)
```

Output
C:\Users\Pro>demo.py 5.25

2.5 Strings.

What is String?

Any sequence of characters within either single quotes or double quotes is considered as a String.

Syntax:
s='Wardha'
s="Wardha"

Note: In most of other languages like C, C++, Java a single character with in single quotes is treated as char data type value. But in Python we are not having char data type. Hence it is treated as String only.

Eg:
```
>>> ch='a'
>>> type(ch)
<class 'str'>
```

How to define multi-line String literals:

We can define multi-line String literals by using triple single or double quotes.

Eg:
```
>>> s="india is
        Great"
```

How to access characters of a String

We can access characters of a string by using the following ways.
1. By using index
2. By using slice operator

1. By using index:

Python supports both +ve and -ve index. +ve index means left to right(Forward direction) -ve index means right to left(Backward direction)

Example:
```
>>> s='ajay'
>>> s[0]
'a'
>>> s[3]
'y'
>>> s[-1]
'y'
>>> s[10]
IndexError: string index out of range
```

Note: If we are trying to access characters of a string with out of range index then we will get error.

```
s=input("Enter Some String:")
i=0
for x in s:
    print(x)
```

Output

```
Enter Some String: Ajay
A
j
a
y
```

2. Accessing characters by using slice operator:

Syntax: s[beginindex:endindex:step]

beginindex: From where we have to consider slice(substring)
endindex: We have to terminate the slice(substring) at endindex-1
step: incremented value

Note: If we are not specifying begin index then it will consider from beginning of the string. If we are not specifying end index then it will consider up to end of the string. The default value for step is 1

Example:

```
>>> s="Learning Python is very very easy!!!"
>>> s[1:7:1]
'earnin'

>>> s[1:7]
'earnin'

>>> s[1:7:2]
'eri'
```

```
>>> s[:]
'Learning Python is very very easy!!!'
>>> s[::-1]
'!!!ysae yrev yrev si nohtyP gninraeL'
```

Behaviour of slice operator:

s[begin:end:step]
step value can be either +ve or –ve

if +ve then it should be forward direction(left to right) and we have to consider begin to end-1

if -ve then it should be backward direction(right to left) and we have to consider begin to end+1

Mathematical Operators for String:

We can apply the following mathematical operators for Strings.
1. + operator for concatenation
2. * operator for repetition

print("soft"+"ware") #software
print("India"*2) #IndiaIndia

Note:
1. To use + operator for Strings, compulsory both arguments should be str type

2. To use * operator for Strings, compulsory one argument should be str and other argument should be int

len() in-built function:

We can use len() function to find the number of characters present in the string.

Eg:
s='ajay'
print(len(s)) #4

Checking Membership: in and not in operators

We can check whether the character or string is the member of another string or not by using in and not in operators.

Program:

```
s=input("Enter main string:")
x=input("Enter string to search")

if x in s:
        print(x," is found in main string")
else:
        print(x,"  is not found in main string")
```

Output:

```
Enter main string: softwaresolutions

Enter string to search: soft
soft is found in main string
```

Comparison of Strings:

We can use comparison operators (<,<=,>,>=) and equality operators(==,!=) for strings.

Comparison will be performed based on alphabetical order.

Example:

```
s1=input("Enter first string:")
s2=input("Enter Second string:")

if s1==s2:
    print("Both strings are equal")
elif s1<s2:
    print("First String is less than Second String")
else:
    print("First String is greater than Second String")
```

Output:

```
Enter first string:India
Enter Second string:Wardha

First String is less than Second String
```

Removing spaces from the string:

We can use the following 3 methods
1. rstrip() ➜To remove spaces at right hand side
2. lstrip() ➜To remove spaces at left hand side
3. strip() ➜To remove spaces both sides

Example:

```
city=input("Enter your city Name:")
x=city.strip()

if x=='Hyderabad':
    print("Hello Hyderbadi..Adab")

elif x=='Chennai':
    print("Hello Madrasi...Vanakkam")

elif x=="Bangalore":
    print("Hello Kannadiga...Shubhodaya")

else:
    print("your entered city is invalid")
```

Output

```
Enter your city Name:Bangalore
Hello Kannadiga...Shubhodaya
```

Finding Substrings

We can use the following 4 methods

For forward direction:
find()
index()

For backward direction:
rfind()
rindex()

1.**find():**

s.find(substring)

Returns index of first occurrence of the given substring. If it is not available then we will get -1
Example:

```
s="Learning Python is very easy"

print(s.find("Python")) #9

print(s.find("Java")) # -1

print(s.find("r"))#3

print(s.rfind("r"))#21
```

Note: By default find() method can search total string. We can also specify the boundaries to search.

s.find(substring,begin,end)

It will always search from begin index to end-1 index

Example:

```
s="wardhacity"

print(s.find('a'))
print(s.find('a',3,15))
print(s.find('z',7,15))
```

Output

```
1
5
-1
```

index() method:

index() method is exactly same as find() method except that if the specified substring is not available then we will get ValueError.

Example:

```
s=input("Enter main string:")
subs=input("Enter sub string:")

n=s.index(subs)
print(n)
```

Output:

```
Enter main string:wardha
Enter sub string:ar
1

Enter main string:wardha
Enter sub string:ra

ValueError: substring not found
```

Counting substring in the given String:

We can find the number of occurrences of substring present in the given string by using count() method.

s.count(substring) ➔ It will search through out the string

Example:

```
s="i am proud of india"

print(s.count('i'))
print(s.count('in'))
print(s.count('ni'))
```

Output:

```
3
1
0
```

Replacing a string with another string:

s.replace(oldstring,newstring)

inside s, every occurrence of oldstring will be replaced with newstring.

Example:

```
s="Learning Python is very difficult"
s1=s.replace("difficult","easy")
print(s1)
print(s)
```

Output:

```
Learning Python is very easy
Learning Python is very difficult
```

Example: All occurrences will be replaced

```
s="ababababababab"
s1=s.replace("a","b")
print(s1)
```

Output:

```
bbbbbbbbbbbbbb
```

Splitting of Strings:

We can split the given string according to specified seperator by using split() method.

l=s.split(seperator)

The default separator is space. The return type of split () method is List

Example 1:

```
s="India is great"

x=s.split()

print(x[0])
print(x[1])
print(x[2])

print('---------------')

for i in x:
    print(i)
```

Output:

```
India
is
great
---------------
India
is
great
```

Joining Strings:

We can join a group of strings (list or tuple) with respect to the given separator.

s=separator. join (group of strings)

Example:

```
l=['hyderabad','singapore','london','dubai']

s=':'.join(l)
print(s)
```

Output

hyderabad:singapore:london:dubai

Changing case of a String:

We can change case of a string by using the following 4 methods.

upper() : To convert all characters to upper case

lower() :To convert all characters to lower case

swapcase() : converts all lower case characters to upper case and all upper case characters to lower case

title() : To convert all character to title case. i.e first character in every word should be upper case and all remaining characters should be in lower case.

capitalize(): Only first character will be converted to upper case and all remaining characters can be converted to lower case

Example:

```
s='learning Python is very Easy'

print(s.upper())
print(s.lower())
print(s.swapcase())
print(s.title())
print(s.capitalize())
```

Output:

```
LEARNING PYTHON IS VERY EASY
learning python is very easy
LEARNING pYTHON IS VERY eASY
Learning Python Is Very Easy
Learning python is very easy
```

Checking starting and ending part of the string:

Python contains the following methods for this purpose

1. s.startswith(substring)
2. s.endswith(substring)

Example:

```
s='learning Python is very easy'

print(s.startswith('learning'))
print(s.endswith('learning'))

print(s.endswith('easy'))
```

Output:

```
True
False
True
```

String formatting in Python

String formatting in Python allows you to create formatted strings by embedding values into placeholders within a string. There are several ways to achieve string formatting in Python:

Old Style Formatting (% operator):
This method uses the % operator to insert values into a string.

```
name = "Ajay"
age = 20
print("My name is %s and I am %d years old" % (name, age))
```

output

Here, %s is a placeholder for a string, and %d is a placeholder for an integer.

String Format Method:

The str.format() method allows you to format strings by using placeholders.

```
name = "Bobby"
height = 185.5
print( "My name is {} and  height is {} cm".format(name, height))
```

Output

My name is Bobby and my score is 185.5 cm

The curly braces {} are used as placeholders.

f-strings (Formatted String Literals):

f-strings provide a concise and readable way to format strings using embedded expressions.

```
name = "rahul"
score = 95
print( f"My name is {name} and my score is {score}")
```

output

My name is rahul and my score is 95

The f prefix indicates that the string is an f-string, and expressions within {} are evaluated and embedded.

2.6 Summary.

Functions can accept different types of arguments, including positional, keyword, default, and variable-length arguments. The scope of a variable refers to the region of the code where the variable is accessible, which can be local or global, while the lifetime of a variable is the duration for which it exists in memory.

Commonly used modules in Python, such as math, random, and sys, provide additional functionalities and tools to enhance programming capabilities. Command line arguments allow users to pass parameters to programs at runtime, enabling dynamic input handling. Strings, a fundamental data type, represent sequences of characters and come with a variety of methods for manipulation and formatting, making them essential for handling textual data.

2.7 Questions.

Multiple Choice Questions

1.Which of the following is NOT a built-in function in Python?

a) len()   b) print()   c) append()   d) input()

2.What type of argument is passed to a function if it is specified without any specific keyword?

a) Positional argument   b) Keyword argument   c) Default argument   d) Variable-length argument

3.In Python, what is the scope of a variable declared inside a function?

a) Global   b) Local   c) Non-local   d) Static

4.Which module in Python is commonly used to interact with the operating system?

a) math   b) sys   c) os   d) random

5.How can you access command line arguments in a Python script?

a) Using the sys module b) Using the os module

c) Using the input() function   d) Using the cmd module

Long Answer Questions

1. Discuss the role and importance of built-in functions in programming languages.

2. Explain the different types of arguments that can be passed to a function in

   Python.

3. Define the concepts of scope and lifetime of variables in Python.

4. Identify and describe some commonly used modules in Python.

5. Explain the process of handling command line arguments in Python.

3.

Advanced data structures.

Unit Structure

3.0 List

3.1 Tuples

3.2 Dictionaries

3.3 Advanced list processing

3.4 Sorting

3.5 Histogram

3.6 Summary

3.7 Questions

3.9 References

3.0 Lists.

Python List

List are used to stores data of homogeneous and heterogenous data. List is sequential. Since Python lists are mutable, we can change their elements after forming. A list is a collection of items separated by commas and denoted by the symbol [].

```python
# a simple list
A = [1, 2, "Python", "Program", 15.9]
B = ["Ajay", "Raj", "Harsh", "Esha"]

print(A)
print(B)

print(type(A))
print(type(B))
```

Output:

```
[1, 2, 'Python', 'Program', 15.9]
['Ajay', 'Raj', 'Harsh', 'Esha']
<class 'list'>
<class 'list'>
```

Characteristics of Lists
- The order is preserved.
- The list element can be accessed via the index.
- The list is mutable
- Elements in the list are similar or dissimilar types.
- List can be compared based on relational operators.

```
a = [ 1, 2, "Ram", 3.50, "Rahul", 5, 6 ]
b = [ 1, 2, 5, "Ram", 3.50, "Rahul", 6 ]
c=a == b
d=a!=b
print(c)
print(d)
```

Output:

```
False
True
```

Program

```
stud= [ "Prashant", 52, "Wardha"]
branch = [ "CS"]

print(" Name : %s, Rollno: %d, City: %s" %(stud[0], stud[1], stud[2]))
print("Branch %s"%( branch[0]) )

print(type (stud),type(branch))
```

Output:

```
Name : Prashant, Rollno: 52, City: Wardha
```

List Indexing and Splitting

The slice operator [] can be used to get to the List's components.
The index ranges from 0 to length -1. The 0th index is where the List's first element is stored; the 1st index is where the second element is stored, and so on.

list_variable(start:stop:step)

- The start parameter is the initial index, the step is the ending index, and the value of the end parameter is the number of elements that are "stepped" through.
- The default value for the step is one without a specific value. The first element in a list appears to have an index of zero.

Consider the following example:

```python
list = [1,2,3,4,5,6,7]
print(list[0])
print(list[1])
print(list[2])
print(list[3])

# Slicing the elements
print(list[0:6])

print(list[:])
print(list[2:5])
print(list[1:6:2])
```

Output:

```
1
2
3
4
[1, 2, 3, 4, 5, 6]
[1, 2, 3, 4, 5, 6, 7]
[3, 4, 5]
[2, 4, 6]
```

Python allows forward and reverse indexing. The negative indices are counted from the right. The index -1 represents the final element on the List's right side, followed by the index -2 for the next member on the left, and so on, until the last element on the left is reached.

```python
list = [1,2,3,4,5]
print(list[-1])
print(list[-3:])
print(list[:-1])
print(list[-3:-1])
```

Output:

```
5
[3, 4, 5]
[1, 2, 3, 4]
[3, 4]
```

updating list values: It is possible to add or update the item in the list.

```
list = [1, 2, 3, 4, 5, 6]
print(list)
list[2] = 10
print(list)
list[1:3] = [89, 78]
print(list)
list[-1] = 25
print(list)
```

Output:

```
[1, 2, 3, 4, 5, 6]
[1, 2, 10, 4, 5, 6]
[1, 89, 78, 4, 5, 6]
[1, 89, 78, 4, 5, 25]
```

The list elements can also be deleted by using the del keyword. Python also provides remove() method if we do not know which element is to be deleted from the list.

```
list = [1, 2, 3, 4, 5, 6]

print(list)
list.remove(3)#item 3 is removed1 2 4 5 6
print(list)
del list[1]#item at index 2 get deleted1 4 5 6
print(list)
list.pop(2)#item at index2 get deleted1 4 6
print(list)
```

Output:

```
[1, 2, 3, 4, 5, 6]
[1, 2, 4, 5, 6]
[1, 4, 5, 6]
[1, 4, 6]
```

Python List Operations

The different operations of the list are

1. Repetition: * is used for repetition operator in list
2. Concatenation: + is used to concatenate. It concatenates the list mentioned on either side of the operator.
3. Length: It is used to get the length of the list
4. Iteration: The for loop is used to iterate over the list elements.
5. Membership: It returns true if a particular item exists in a particular list otherwise false.

```python
list1 = [12, 14, 16, 18, 20]
list2 = [9, 10, 32, 54, 86]
l = list1 * 2
print(l)
l = list1 + list2
print(l)
len(list1)
for i in list1:
    print(i)
list3 = [100, 200, 300, 400, 500]
print(200 in list3)
print(700 in list3)
```

output

```
[12, 14, 16, 18, 20, 12, 14, 16, 18, 20]
[12, 14, 16, 18, 20, 9, 10, 32, 54, 86]
12
14
```

16
18
20
True
False

Adding Elements to the List

The append() function in Python can add a new item to the List.

```
l =[]

n = int(input("Enter the number of elements in the list:"))

for i in range(0,n):
    x=int(input('enter item'))
    l.append(x)

print("printing the list items..")

for i in l:
    print(i, end = " ")
```

Output:

```
Enter the number of elements in the list:3
enter item8
enter item5
enter item3
printing the list items..
```

Python List Built-in Functions

max() : It returns the maximum element of the list
min():it returns the minimum element of the list
len( ) : It is used to calculate the length of the list.

```
list1 = [12, 16, 18, 20, 39, 40]
print(len(list1)  )
```

```
list2 = [103, 675, 321, 782, 200]
print(max(list1))
list3 = [103, 675, 321, 782, 200]
print(min(list3))
```

output

```
6
40
103
```

3.1   Tuples.

Python Tuples

Tuples cannot alter the components they have been assigned.

Features of Python Tuple

- Tuples are an immutable data type, meaning their elements cannot be changed after they are generated.
- Each element in a tuple has a specific order that will never change because tuples are ordered sequences.
- All "elements"-must be separated by a comma, enclosed in parenthesis ().
- Items can be of various data types (dictionary, string, float, list, etc.), can be contained in a tuple.

```
t = ()
print("Empty tuple: ",t)

t1 = (4, 6, 8, 10, 12, 14)
print("Tuple with integers: ",t1)

t2 = (4, "Python", 9.3)
print("Tuple with different data types: ", t2)
```

```python
t3 = ("Python", {4: 5, 6: 2, 8: 2}, (5, 3, 5, 6))
print("A nested tuple: ", t3)
```

Output:

```
Empty tuple:  ()
Tuple with integers:  (4, 6, 8, 10, 12, 14)
Tuple with different data types:  (4, 'Python', 9.3)
A nested tuple:  ('Python', {4: 5, 6: 2, 8: 2}, (5, 3, 5, 6))
```

Accessing Tuple Elements

A tuple's objects can be accessed in a variety of ways.

Indexing : We can use the index operator [] to access an object in a tuple, where the index starts at 0. The indices of a tuple with five items will range from 0 to 4.

```python
t = ("Ram","Ajay")
print(t[0], "\n",t[1])
```

Output:

```
Ram
Ajay
```

Negative Indexing

Python's sequence objects support negative indexing. The last thing of the assortment is addressed by - 1, the second last thing by - 2, etc.

```python
t = ("Wardha","Nagpur","Mumbai","Bangalore")

print("Element at -1 index: ", t[-1])
print("Elements between -4 and -1 are: ", t[-4:-1])
```

Output:

```
Element at -1 index:  Bangalore
Elements between -4 and -1 are:  ('Wardha', 'Nagpur', 'Mumbai')
```

Slicing

To gain access to various tuple elements, we can use the slicing operator colon (:).

```python
A = ("Ajay","Jay","Vijay","Amay","Sanjay")
print("1 and 3: ", A[1:3])
print(" 0 and -4: ", A[:-4])
print("Entire tuple: ",A[:])
```

Output:

```
1 and 3:  ('Jay', 'Vijay')
 0 and -4:  ('Ajay',)
Entire tuple:  ('Ajay', 'Jay', 'Vijay', 'Amay', 'Sanjay')
```

Deleting a Tuple

A tuple's parts can't be modified, as was recently said. We are unable to eliminate or remove tuple components as a result. However, the keyword del can completely delete a tuple.

```python
A = ("Ajay","Jay","Vijay","Amay","Sanjay")
print(A)
del A
```

output

('Ajay', 'Jay', 'Vijay', 'Amay', 'Sanjay')

Repetition Tuples in Python

```python
t = ('Python',"Java")
print(t)
t=t*3
print("New tuple is: ", t)
```

Output:

```
('Python', 'Java')
New tuple is:  ('Python', 'Java', 'Python', 'Java', 'Python', 'Java')
```

Tuple Methods:

Count () Method: Tuple is returned by the count () capability of the Tuple.

```
T1 = (0, 1, 5, 6, 7, 2, 2, 4, 2, 3, 2, 3, 1, 3, 2)
T2 = ('python', 'java', 'python', 'Program', 'python', 'java')
res = T1.count(2)
print('Count of 2  is:', res)
res = T2.count('java')
print('Count of Java  is:', res)
```

Output:

```
Count of 2 is: 5
Count of java is: 2
```

Index() Method: The Index() function returns the first instance of the requested element from the Tuple.

Start: (Optional) the index that is used to begin the final (optional) search: The most recent index from which the search is carried out

```
td = (0, 1, 2, 3, 2, 3, 1, 3, 2)
res = td.index(3)
print('First index of 1 is', res)
res = td.index(3, 4)
print('First index of 1 after 4th index is:', res)
```

Output:

```
First index of 1 is 2
First index of 1 after 4th index is: 6
```

Tuple Membership Test

We can decide whether a thing is available in the given Tuple.

Iterating Through a Tuple

A for loop can be used to iterate through each tuple element

```
t=(3,5,4,2,6,2,6)
print(4  in t)
print(5 in t)
print(7  not in  t)
print(2 not  in t)
print('Tuple Items')
for item in t:
    print(item,end=' ')
```

Output:

```
True
True
True
False
Tuple Items
3 5 4 2 6 2 6
```

The + operator can be used to combine multiple tuples into one. This phenomenon is known as concatenation. We can also repeat the elements of a tuple a predetermined number of times by using the * operator.

```
tt=("Hello","fine","ok")
print(tt + (4, 5, 6))
print(tt *2)
```

Output:

> ('Hello', 'fine', 'ok', 4, 5, 6)
> ('Hello', 'fine', 'ok', 'Hello', 'fine', 'ok')

Advantages of tuples over list

- Tuples are faster than lists.
- Tuples make the code safe from any accidental modification. If a data is needed in a program which is not supposed to be changed, then it is better to put it in 'tuples' than in 'list'.
- Tuples can be used as dictionary keys if it contains immutable values like strings, numbers or another tuple. 'Lists' can never be used as dictionary keys as 'lists' are mutable.

3.2 Dictionaries.

Python Dictionary

Dictionaries are a useful data structure for storing data in Python where a certain value exists for a given key. The data is stored as key-value pairs using a Python dictionary.

- This data structure is mutable
- The components of dictionary were made using keys and values.
- Keys must only have one component.
- Values can be of any type, including integer, list, and tuple.
- dictionaries are generally unordered.

Creating the Dictionary

Curly brackets {} are used to creating a dictionary with key-values, and a colon separating each key from its value.

Syntax:
Dict = {"Name": "Sachin", "Age": 25}

The keys Name and Age are the strings which comes under the category of an immutable object.

```
Student = {"Name": "Ajay", "Age": 21, "Percent":96,"Branch":"IT"}
print(type(Student))
print("Student details are ")
print(Student)
```

Output

```
<class 'dict'>
Student details are
{"Name": "Ajay", "Age": 21, "Percent":96,"Branch":"IT"}
```

Accessing the dictionary values

To access data contained in lists and tuples, indexing has been studied. The keys of the dictionary can be used to obtain the values because they are unique from one another. The following method can be used to access dictionary values.

```
e = {"Name": "Ajay", "Age": 20, "salary":45000}
print(type(e))
print('Employee Details')
print("Name = ",e["Name"])
print("Age = ",e["Age"])
print("Salary = ",e["salary"])
```

Output

```
<class 'dict'>
Employee Details
Name =  Ajay
Age =  20
Salary =  45000
```

Adding Dictionary Values

The dictionary is a mutable data type, and utilising the right keys allows you to change its values. Dict[key] = value and the value can both be modified. An existing value can also be updated using the update() method.

Pop() : The value connected to a specific key in a dictionary is removed using the pop() method, which then returns the value. The key of the element to be removed is the only argument needed.

```
A = {}
print("Empty Dictionary: ")
print(A)

A[0]="Ajay"
A[1]="Sanjay"
A[2]="Vijay"
print(A)

A['more']=45,65,33
print(A)

A[3]=98
print("\nUpdated key value: ")
print(A)
del A[0]
print(A)
d = A.pop(2)#delete a key
print(d)
print(A)

print("Deleting the dictionary");
del A
```

Output

```
Empty Dictionary:
{}
{0: 'Ajay', 1: 'Sanjay', 2: 'Vijay'}
{0: 'Ajay', 1: 'Sanjay', 2: 'Vijay', 'more': (45, 65, 33)}
```

Updated key value:
{0: 'Ajay', 1: 'Sanjay', 2: 'Vijay', 'more': (45, 65, 33), 3: 98}
{1: 'Sanjay', 2: 'Vijay', 'more': (45, 65, 33), 3: 98}
Vijay
{1: 'Sanjay', 'more': (45, 65, 33), 3: 98}

Deleting the dictionary

Iterating Dictionary

A dictionary can be iterated using for loop.
Values() : It is used to print the values of the dictionary by using values() method
Items() :It is used to print the items of the dictionary by using items() method

```python
e = {"Name": "Ajay", "Age": 29, "salary":25000}
for x in e:
    print(x,":",e[x])
print('--------\nOnly Values')
for x in e.values():
    print(x, end = ' ')
print('\n--------------\nPrint Items')
for x in e.items():
    print(x)
```

Output

```
Name : Ajay
Age : 29
salary : 25000
--------
Only Values
Ajay  29  25000
--------------
Print Items
('Name', 'Ajay')
('Age', 29)
('salary', 25000)
```

Built-in Dictionary Functions

len() : The dictionary's length is returned via the len() function in Python. The string is lengthened by one for each key-value pair.

copy() :It returns a shallow copy of the dictionary which is created.

pop() :It mainly eliminates the element using the defined key.

popitem() : removes the most recent key-value pair entered

keys() : It returns all the keys of the dictionary.

get() :It is used to get the value specified for the passed key

sorted(): the sorted() method returns an ordered series of the dictionary's keys.

clear() :It is mainly used to delete all the items of the dictionary.

update() :It mainly updates all the dictionary by adding the key-value pair.

```python
d1 = {2: "WIPRO", 1: "Facebook", 4: "Amazon", 5: "Flipkart"}
print("length = ",len(d1)) #print the length
print("sorted = ",sorted(d1)) #sorted the items key wise

d3 = d1.copy()   #copy the dictionary
print("copied dictionary =",d3)

x = d1.pop(1)   #remove the item of key 1
print("deleted item =",x)

print(d1.keys())#prints keys
print(d1.get(3))

d1.update({3: "Persistence"})
print(d1)
d1.clear()#clear the dictionary
print(d1)
```

Output

```
length =  4
sorted =  [1, 2, 4, 5]
copied dictionary = {5: 'Flipkart', 2: 'WIPRO', 1: 'Facebook', 4: 'Amazon'}
deleted item = Facebook
dict_keys([5, 2, 4])
None
{5: 'Flipkart', 2: 'WPRO', 4: 'Amazon', 3: 'Persistence'}
{}
```

3.3 List Comprehension

Python List Comprehension

A Python list comprehension consists of brackets containing the expression, which is executed for each element along with the for loop to iterate over each element in the Python list.

Syntax:

newlist = [expression for item in iterable if condition == True]

```
#using for loop to iterate through items in list
numbers = [3, 5, 1, 7, 3, 9]
num = []
 for n in numbers:
    num.append(n**2)
 print(num)
```

Output:
```
[9, 25, 1, 49, 9, 81]
```

This can be accomplished with only a single line of code using list comprehension.

```
numbers = [3, 5, 1, 7, 3, 9]
num = [n**2 for n in numbers]

print(num)
```

Output:

```
[9, 25, 1, 49, 9, 81]
```

Lambda Functions

Lambda functions can create and modify lists in less lines of code. A lambda function is a small anonymous function. A lambda function can take any number of arguments, but can only have one expression.

Syntax

lambda arguments : expression
The expression is executed and the result is returned:

Without Using Lambda functions

```
def abc(n):
        x=n+10
        return x

y=abc(5)
print(y)
```

Using Lambda functions

Add 10 to argument a, and return the result:

```
x = lambda a : a + 10
print(x(5))
```

Output

```
15
```

Using Lambda functions inside List

```
letters = list(map(lambda x: x, 'human'))
print(letters)
```

output

```
['h','u','m','a','n']
```

Using List Comprehension to Iterate through String

List comprehension can also be used in the case of strings, as they are iterables.
Without using list comprehension

```
letters =  'Welcome Python'
for i in letters:
    print( i,end=' ')
```

```
letters = [ i for i in 'Welcome Python' ]
print( letters)
```

Output

```
['W', 'e', 'l', 'c', 'o', 'm', 'e', ' ', 'P', 'y', 't', 'h', 'o', 'n']
```

Using Conditions in List Comprehension

Conditional statements can be used by list comprehensions to change existing lists (or other tuples).

```
num_list = [4, 11, 2, 19, 7, 6, 25, 12]
new_list = [num for num in num_list if num > 10]
print(new_list)
```

Output:

```
[11, 19, 25, 12]
```


3.4 Sorting

1. SELECTION SORT PROGRAM

- The selection sort algorithm sorts an array by repeatedly finding the minimum element (considering ascending order) from unsorted part and putting it at the beginning.
- The provided Python code demonstrates the Selection Sort algorithm. Selection Sort has a time complexity of O(n^2).
- In each iteration, the code finds the minimum element's index in the unsorted portion of the array and swaps it with the current index's element. This gradually sorts the array from left to right.

```python
a = [34,56,32,75,23,65]
n=len(a)
print('The array before sorting :')
for i in range(n):
   print(a[i],end=' ')
for i in range(n):
     for j in range(i+1):
        if(a[i]<a[j]):
           t=a[i];
           a[i]=a[j]
           a[j]=t

print('\nThe array after sorting :')
for i in range(n):
   print(a[i],end=' ')
```

Output

```
The array before sorting :
34 56 32 75 23 65
The array after sorting :
23 32 34 56 65 75
```

2. INSERTION SORT PROGRAM

The insertion Sort function takes an array arr as input. It first calculates the length of the array (n). If the length is 0 or 1, the function returns immediately as an array with 0 or 1 element is considered already sorted.

For arrays with more than one element, the function proceeds to iterate over the array starting from the second element. It takes the current element (referred to as the "key") and compares it with the elements in the sorted portion of the array that precede it.

If the key is smaller than an element in the sorted portion, the function shifts that element to the right, creating space for the key. This process continues until the correct position for the key is found, and it is then inserted in that position.

```python
def insertionSort(arr):
    n = len(arr)

    if n <= 1:
        return

    for i in range(1, n):
        key = arr[i]
        j = i - 1
        while j >= 0 and key < arr[j]:
            arr[j + 1] = arr[j]
            j -= 1
        arr[j + 1] = key

arr = [12, 11, 13, 5, 6]
insertionSort(arr)
print(arr)
```

Output

```
12, 11, 13, 5, 6
5, 6, 11, 12, 13
```

3. MERGE SORT PROGRAM

The provided Python code implements the Merge Sort algorithm, a divide-and-conquer sorting technique. It breaks down an array into smaller subarrays, sorts them individually, and then merges them back together to create a sorted array.
The code includes two main functions: merge, responsible for merging two subarrays, and mergeSort, which recursively divides and sorts the array.

The merge function combines two sorted subarrays into a single sorted array. The mergeSort function recursively splits the array in half until each subarray has a single element, then merges them to achieve the final sorted result.

```python
def merge(arr, l, m, r):
    n1 = m - l + 1
    n2 = r - m

    # create temp arrays
    L = [0] * (n1)
    R = [0] * (n2)

    for i in range(0, n1):
        L[i] = arr[l + i]

    for j in range(0, n2):
        R[j] = arr[m + 1 + j]

    i = 0
    j = 0
    k = l

    while i < n1 and j < n2:
        if L[i] <= R[j]:
            arr[k] = L[i]
            i += 1
```

```python
        else:
            arr[k] = R[j]
            j += 1
        k += 1

    while i < n1:
        arr[k] = L[i]
        i += 1
        k += 1

    while j < n2:
        arr[k] = R[j]
        j += 1
        k += 1

def mergeSort(arr, l, r):
    if l < r:

        m = l+(r-l)//2

        mergeSort(arr, l, m)
        mergeSort(arr, m+1, r)
        merge(arr, l, m, r)

arr = [12, 11, 13, 5, 6, 7]
n = len(arr)
print("Given array is")
for i in range(n):
    print("%d" % arr[i],end=" ")

mergeSort(arr, 0, n-1)
print("\n\nSorted array is")
for i in range(n):
    print("%d" % arr[i],end=" ")
```

output

Given array is
12 11 13 5 6 7
Sorted array is
5 6 7 11 12 13

3.5 Histogram

To create a histogram the first step is to create bin of the ranges, then distribute the whole range of the values into a series of intervals and count the values which fall into each of the intervals. The matplotlib. pyplot.hist() function is used to compute and create histogram of x.

The different parameters of matplotlib are:

Attribute   parameter

x   array or sequence of array

bins   optional parameter contains integer or sequence or strings

density   optional parameter contains boolean values

range   optional parameter represents upper and lower range of bins

histtype optional parameter used to create type of histogram [bar, barstacked, step, stepfilled], default is "bar"

align   optional parameter controls the plotting of histogram [left, right, mid]

weights   optional parameter contains array of weights having same dimensions as x

bottom   location of the baseline of each bin

Attribute	parameter
rwidth	optional parameter which is relative width of the bars with respect to bin width
color	optional parameter used to set color or sequence of color specs
label	optional parameter string or sequence of string to match with multiple datasets
log	optional parameter used to set histogram axis on log scale

Program

```
from matplotlib import pyplot as plt
import numpy as np

# Creating dataset
a = np.array([22, 87, 5, 43, 56,
        73, 55, 54, 11,
        20, 51, 5, 79, 31,
        27])

# Creating histogram
fig, ax = plt.subplots(figsize =(10, 7))
ax.hist(a, bins = [0, 25, 50, 75, 100])

# Show plot
plt.show()
```

Output

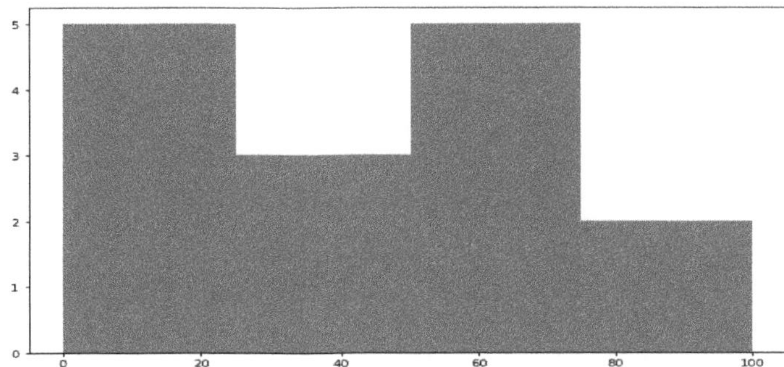

Program

```python
import matplotlib.pyplot as plt
import numpy as np
from matplotlib import colors
from matplotlib.ticker import PercentFormatter

# Creating dataset
np.random.seed(2)
N_points = 10000
n_bins = 20

# Creating distribution
x = np.random.randn(N_points)
y = .8 ** x + np.random.randn(10000) + 25

# Creating histogram
fig, axs = plt.subplots(1, 1,
                figsize =(10, 7),
                tight_layout = True)

axs.hist(x, bins = n_bins)

# Show plot
plt.show()
```

Output

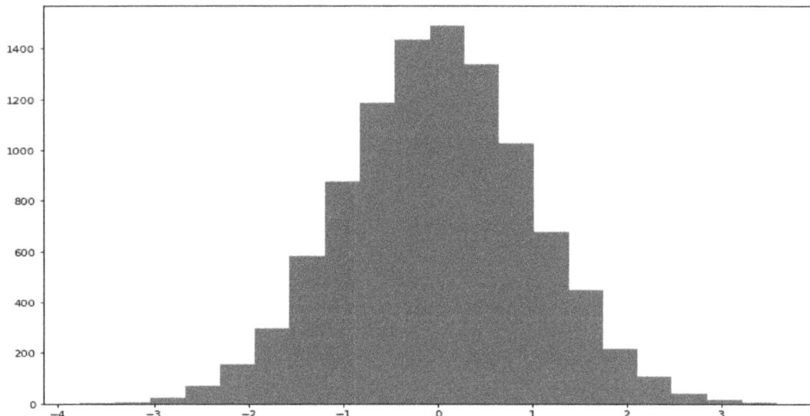

3.6 Summary.

Lists in Python are versatile and mutable sequences used to store collections of items. They support various operations such as indexing, slicing, and a wide range of methods like append(), extend(), and remove(). List slices allow accessing subsets of a list, enabling powerful data manipulation. Looping through lists can be done using for or while loops, facilitating iteration over each element.

Tuples are immutable sequences that support tuple assignment and can be used as return values from functions. Their immutability makes them ideal for fixed collections of items.

Dictionaries are key-value pairs that offer efficient data retrieval and support operations like adding, removing, and modifying elements, along with methods such as get(), keys(), and values(). Advanced list processing techniques like list comprehension provide a concise way to create lists based on existing lists. Illustrative programs demonstrate the practical applications of these data structures, such as sorting algorithms (selection sort, insertion sort, merge sort) and generating histograms to visualize data distributions.

3.8 Questions.

Multiple Choice Questions

1.Which of the following is a method used to add an element to the end of a list in Python?
a) insert()   b) append()   c) extend()   d) add()

2.What will be the output of the following code snippet? list = [1, 2, 3, 4]; print(list[1:3])
a) [1, 2]   b) [2, 3]   c) [2, 3, 4]   d) [1, 2, 3]

3.Which of the following statements about tuples is true?
a) Tuples are mutable.
b) Tuples cannot be used as keys in dictionaries.
c) Tuples support assignment and can be returned from functions.
d) Tuples have fewer methods compared to lists because they are immutable.

4.How can you create a dictionary in Python?
a) dict = {1, 2, 3}   b) dict = [key1: value1, key2: value2]
c) dict = {key1: value1, key2: value2} d) dict = (key1: value1, key2: value2)
5.What is the primary advantage of using list comprehensions in Python?
a) They increase the execution time of a program.
b) They provide a more readable and concise way to create lists.
c) They prevent errors in list operations.
d) They make lists immutable.

Long Answer Questions

1) Explain the concept of list slicing in Python.
2) Discuss the mutability of lists in Python and the implications of aliasing.
3) Describe the tuple data structure in Python.
4) Provide a detailed overview of dictionary operations and methods in Python.
5) Explain the concept of list comprehension in Python.

4.

Files & Exception

Unit Structure

4.0 Text files, reading and writing files

4.1 Errors and exceptions,

4.2 Handling exceptions

4.3 Illustrative programs

4.4 Summary

4.5 Questions

4.6 References

4.0 Exception

An unwanted and unexpected event that disturbs normal flow of program is called exception.

The main objective of exception handling is Graceful Termination of the program. Exception handling does not mean repairing exception. We have to define alternative way to continue rest of the program normally.

In any programming language there are 2 types of errors are possible.

1. Syntax Errors
2. Runtime Errors

1. Syntax Errors:

The errors which occur because of invalid syntax are called syntax errors.

```
x=10

if x=10 :
    print("Hello")
```

Output

```
SyntaxError: invalid syntax
```

The programmer is responsible to correct these syntax errors. Once all syntax errors are corrected then only program execution will be started.

2. Runtime Errors (Exceptions)

While executing the program if something goes wrong because of end user input or programming logic or memory problems etc. then we will get Runtime Errors.

Example:

```
print(10/0) →ZeroDivisionError: division by zero
print(10/"ten") →TypeError: unsupported operand type(s) for /: 'int' and 'str'
```

```
x=int(input("Enter Number:"))

print(x)
```

Output

```
Enter Number:ten
ValueError: invalid literal for int() with base 10: 'ten'
```

Default Exception Handing in Python

Every exception in Python is an object. For every exception type the corresponding classes are available. Whenever an exception occurs python will create the corresponding exception object and will check for handling code.

If handling code is not available then Python interpreter terminates the program abnormally and prints corresponding exception information to the console.

The rest of the program won't be executed.

Example:

```
print("Hello")
print(10/0)
print("Hi")
```

Output

```
Hello
ZeroDivisionError: division by zero
```

Every Exception in Python is a class. All exception classes are child classes of BaseException. i.e every exception class extends BaseException either directly or indirectly.

Customized Exception Handling by using try-except:

It is highly recommended to handle exceptions. The code which may raise exception is called risky code and we have to take risky code inside try block. The corresponding handling code we have to take inside except block.

Syntax

```
try:
        statement
except exception-name:
        statement
```

with try-except:

```
a=int(input('Enter first number'))
b=int(input('Enter second number'))

try:
   c=a/b
   print('Result =',c)

except ZeroDivisionError:
   print("Don't enter second number as zero")
```

Output

```
Enter first number10
Enter second number0
Don't enter second number as zero
```

try with multiple except blocks

The way of handling exception is varied from exception to exception. Hence for every exception type a separate except block we have to provide. i.e try with multiple except blocks is possible and recommended to use.

Example:

```
try:
       -------
       -------
       -------
except Exceptioname:
       -------
except Exceptionname:
       --------
....
```

If try with multiple except blocks available then based on raised exception the corresponding except block will be executed.

Example:

```
try:
    x=int(input("Enter First Number: "))
    y=int(input("Enter Second Number: "))
    print(x/y)

except ZeroDivisionError :
    print("Can't Divide with Zero")

except ValueError:
    print("Please provide int value only")
```

Output

```
Enter First Number: 10
Enter Second Number: 0
Can't Divide with Zero
```

If try with multiple except blocks available then the order of these except blocks is important .Python interpreter will always consider from top to bottom until matched except block identified.

Single except block that can handle multiple exceptions:

We can write a single except block that can handle multiple different types of exceptions.

except (Exception1,Exception2,exception3,..): or
except (Exception1,Exception2,exception3,..) as msg :

Parenthesis are mandatory and this group of exceptions internally considered as tuple.

Example:

```python
try:
    x=int(input("Enter First Number: "))
    y=int(input("Enter Second Number: "))
    print(x/y)

except (ZeroDivisionError,ValueError) as msg:
    print("Please provide valid numbers only and problem is: ",msg)
```

Output

```
Enter First Number: 7
Enter Second Number: 0
Please provide valid numbers only and problem is:  division by zero
```

Default except block

We can use default except block to handle any type of exceptions. In default except block generally we can print normal error messages.

Syntax:

```
except:
        statements
```

Example:

```python
try:
    x=int(input("Enter First Number: "))
    y=int(input("Enter Second Number: "))
    print(x/y)

except ZeroDivisionError:
    print("ZeroDivisionError: Can't divide with zero")

except:
    print("Default Except: Plz provide valid input only")
```

Output

Note: If try with multiple except blocks available then default except block should be last, otherwise we will get SyntaxError.

finally block:

When we required some place to maintain clean up code which should be executed always irrespective of whether exception raised or not raised and whether exception handled or not handled. Such type of best place is nothing but finally block.

Hence the main purpose of finally block is to maintain clean up code.

```
try:
        Risky Code
except:
        Handling Code
finally:
        Cleanup code
```

The specialty of finally block is it will be executed always whether exception raised or not raised and whether exception handled or not handled.

If there is an exception raised but handled:

```
try:
    print("try")
    print(10/0)

except ZeroDivisionError:
    print("except")

finally:
    print("finally")
```

```
try
except
finally
```

else block with try-except-finally:

We can use else block with try-except-finally blocks. else block will be executed if and only if there are no exceptions inside try block.

Syntax:

```
try:
        Risky Code
except:
        will be executed if exception inside try
else:
        will be executed if there is no exception inside try
finally:
        will be executed whether exception raised or not raised and handled or not handled
```

Example:

```
try:
   print("try")
   print(10/0)

except:
   print("except")

else:
   print("else")
finally:
   print("finally")
```

Output

```
try
except
finally
```

4.1   Types of Exception

In Python there are 2 types of exceptions possible.

1. Predefined Exceptions
2. User Defined Exceptions

1. Predefined Exceptions (Built-In exceptions)

The exceptions which are raised automatically by Python virtual machine (PVM), whenever a particular event occurs, are called pre-defined exceptions.

Whenever we are trying to perform Division by zero, automatically Python will raise ZeroDivisionError.
print(10/0)

2. User Defined Exceptions:

It is also known as Customized Exceptions or Programmatic Exceptions. Some time we have to define and raise exceptions explicitly to indicate that something goes wrong, such type of exceptions is called User Defined Exceptions or Customized Exceptions

The programmer is responsible for defining these exceptions. Hence, we must raise explicitly based on our requirement by using "raise" keyword.

How to Define and Raise Customized Exceptions:

Every exception in Python is a class that extends Exception class either directly or indirectly.

Syntax:

```
class classname(predefined exception class name):
        def __init__(self,arg):
            self.msg=arg
```

Example:

We can raise exceptions by using raise keyword as follows raise

TooYoungException("message")

```
class TooYoungException(Exception):
    def __init__(self,arg):
        self.msg=arg
class TooOldException(Exception):
    def __init__(self,arg):
        self.msg=arg

age=int(input("Enter Age:"))
if age>60:
    raise TooOldException("Age Limit!!!You are not eligible for Driving License!")
elif age<18:
    raise TooYoungException("Too Young!!!You are not eligible for Driving License!")
else:
    print("You will get Driving License!")
```

Output

```
Enter Age:20
You will get Driving License!

Enter Age:12
TooYoungException: Too Young!!!You are not eligible for Driving License!

Enter Age:65
TooOldException: Age Limit!!!You are not eligible for Driving License!
```

4.2 File Handling

As a part of programming requirement, we have to store our data permanently for future purpose. For this requirement we should go for files. Files are very common permanent storage areas to store our data.

Types of Files

There are two types of files

1. Text Files: Usually we can use text files to store character data
eg: abc.txt

2. Binary Files: Usually we can use binary files to store binary data like images, video files, audio files etc...

Opening a File:

Before performing any operation (like read or write) on the file, first we have to open that file. For this we should use Python's inbuilt function open(). But at the time of open, we have to specify mode, which represents the purpose of opening file.

f = open(filename, mode)

Modes in Python are

1. r → open an existing file for read operation. The file pointer is positioned at the beginning of the file. If the specified file does not exist then we will get FileNotFoundError. This is default mode

2. w → open an existing file for write operation. If the file already contains some data then it will be overwritten. If the specified file is not already available then this mode will create that file.

3. a → open an existing file for append operation. It won't overwrite existing data. If the specified file is not already available then this mode will create a new file.

4. r+ → To read and write data into the file. The previous data in the file will not be deleted. The file pointer is placed at the beginning of the file.

5. w+ → To write and read data. It will overwrite existing data.

6. a+ → To append and read data from the file. It won't overwrite existing data.

7. x → To open a file in exclusive creation mode for write operation. If the file already exists then we will get FileExistsError.

Note: All the above modes are applicable for text files. If the above modes suffixed with 'b' then these represents for binary files.

Eg: rb,wb,ab,r+b,w+b,a+b,xb

f = open("abc.txt","w")
We are opening abc.txt file for writing data.

Closing a File:

After completing our operations on the file, it is highly recommended to close the file. For this we have to use close() function.

f.close()

Properties of File Object:
Name   **Name of opened file**

mode   Mode in which the file is opened

closed   Returns boolean value indicates that file is closed or not

readable()   Returns boolean value indicates that whether file is readable or not

writable()   Returns boolean value indicates that whether file is writable or not.

Example:

```
f=open("abc.txt",'w')

print("File Name: ",f.name)
print("File Mode: ",f.mode)

print("Is File Readable: ",f.readable())
print("Is File Writable: ",f.writable())
print("Is File Closed : ",f.closed)

f.close()
print("Is File Closed : ",f.closed)
```

Output

```
File Name:  abc.txt
File Mode:  w
Is File Readable:  False
Is File Writable:  True
Is File Closed :  False
Is File Closed :  True
```

Writing data to text files

We can write character data to the text files by using the following two methods.

```
write(str)
writelines(list of lines)
```

Example:

```
f=open("abcd.txt",'w')

f.write("Wardha\n")
f.write("World\n")
f.write("!!!!!!!\n")

print("Data written to the file successfully ")
f.close()
```

Output

```
Data written to the file successfully
```

Note: In the above program, data present in the file will be overwritten every time if we run the program. Instead of overwritten if we want append operation then we should open the file as follows.

f = open("abcd.txt","a")

```
f=open("abcd.txt",'w')
list=["sunny\n","bunny\n","vinny\n","chinny"]

f.writelines(list)
print("List of lines written to the file successfully")

f.close()
```

Output

```
List of lines written to the file successfully
```

Open file abcd.txt:

```
sunny
bunny
vinny
chinny
```

Note: while writing data by using write() methods, compulsory we have to provide line seperator(\n),otherwise total data will be written to a single line.

Reading Character Data from text files:

We can read character data from text file by using the following read methods.

read() → To read total data from the file
read(n)   → To read 'n' characters from the file
readline() → To read only one line
readlines() → To read all lines into a list

Example 1: To read total data from the file

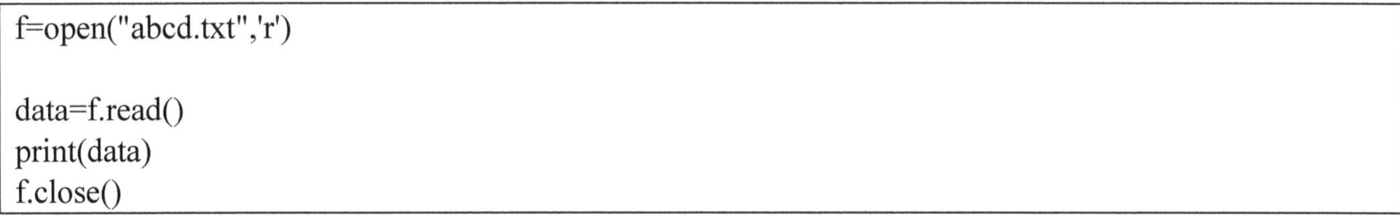

```python
f=open("abcd.txt",'r')

data=f.read()
print(data)
f.close()
```

Output

```
sunny
bunny
chinny
vinny
```

Example 2: To read only first 10 characters:

```python
f=open("abcd.txt",'r')
data=f.read(10)
print(data)
f.close()
```

Output
```
sunny
bunn
```

Example 3: To read data line by line:

```python
f=open("abc.txt",'r')

x=f.readline()
print(x,end='')

y=f.readline()
print(y,end='')

z=f.readline()
print(z,end='')

f.close()
```

Output

```
sunny
bunny
chinny
```

Example 4: To read all lines into list:

```
f=open("abcd.txt",'r')
l=f.readlines()

for x in l:
    print(x,end='')

f.close()
```

Output

```
sunny
bunny
chinny
vinny
```

The seek() and tell() methods:

tell():

We can use tell() method to return current position of the cursor(file pointer) from beginning of the file. The position(index) of first character in files is zero just like string index.

Example:

```
f=open("abc.txt","r")

print(f.tell())
print(f.read(2))

print(f.tell())
print(f.read(3))
print(f.tell())
```

Output:

```
0
hi
2

2
```

seek():

We can use seek() method to move cursor(file pointer) to specified location.

f.seek(offset, fromwhere)
offset represents the number of positions

The allowed values for second attribute(from where) are
0---->From beginning of file(default value)

Example:

```
x="All Students are SMART"

f=open("abc.txt","w")
f.write(x)

with open("abc.txt","r+") as f:

    text=f.read()
    print(text)

    print("The Current Cursor Position: ",f.tell())
    f.seek(17)
    print("The Current Cursor Position: ",f.tell())

    f.write("GEMS!!!")
    f.seek(0)

    text=f.read()
    print("Data After Modification:")
    print(text)
```

Output

```
All Students are SMART
The Current Cursor Position:  22
The Current Cursor Position:  17
Data After Modification:
All Students are GEMS!!!
```

How to check a particular file exists or not?

We can use os library to get information about files in our computer. os module has path sub module, which contains isFile() function to check whether a particular file exists or not?

os.path.isfile(fname)
Program to check whether the given file exists or not. If it is available then print its content.

```python
import os,sys
fname=input("Enter File Name: ")

if os.path.isfile(fname):
    print("File exists:",fname)
    f=open(fname,"r")
else:
    print("File does not exist:",fname)
    sys.exit(0)

print("The content of file is:")
data=f.read()
print(data)
```

Output

```
Enter File Name: abc.txt
File does not exist: abc.txt


Enter File Name: abcd.txt
```

Note:
sys.exit(0) →To exit system without executing rest of the program. argument represents status code . 0 means normal termination and it is the default value.

Working with Directories:

It is very common requirement to perform operations for directories like

1. To know current working directory
2. To create a new directory
3. To remove an existing directory
4. To rename a directory
5. To list contents of the directory

To perform these operations, Python provides inbuilt module os, which contains several functions to perform directory related operations.

To Know Current Working Directory:

```
import os

d=os.getcwd()
print("Current Working Directory:",d)
```

Output

```
Current Working Directory:
C:\Users\Pro\AppData\Local\Programs\Python\Python37-32
```

To create a sub directory in the current working directory:

```
import os

os.mkdir("mysub")
print("mysub directory created in cwd")
```

Output
```
mysub directory created in cwd
```

To remove a directory:

```
import os

os.rmdir("mysub/mysub2")
print("mysub2 directory deleted")
```

Output

```
mysub2 directory deleted
```

To rename a directory:

```
import os
os.rename("mysub","newdir")

print("mysub directory renamed to newdir")
```

Output

```
mysub directory renamed to newdir
```

To know contents of directory:
os module provides listdir() to list out the contents of the specified directory. It won't display the contents of sub directory.

Example:

```
import os
print(os.listdir("."))
```

Output

```
['abc.py', 'abc.txt', 'abcd.txt', 'com', 'demo.py', 'demomath.py', file1.txt, 'file2.txt', 'file3.txt', 'files.zip',
'log.txt', 'module1.py', 'myl og.txt', 'newdir', 'pack1', 'test.py', '__pycache__' ]
```

4.4 Summary.

Errors and exceptions are critical to managing unexpected events in a program. Handling exceptions typically involves using try-except blocks to catch and respond to errors gracefully, preventing the program from crashing.

In programming, text file handling involves reading from and writing to files. This can be done using various methods depending on the language. For instance, in Python, you can use functions like open(), read(), write(), and close() to manipulate text files. Modules and packages organize code into reusable components, making it easier to manage and maintain. A module is a single file containing Python code, while a package is a collection of modules.

4.5 Questions.

Multiple Choice Questions

1. Which function is used to open a file in Python for reading?
A) file.open()   B) open()   C) read()   D) write()

2. What is the format operator in Python that allows formatting of strings?
A) #   B) %   C) @   D) &

3. Which module in Python is used for parsing command line arguments?
A) argparse   B) sys   C) getopt   D) os

4. Which of the following is NOT a type of error in Python?
A) SyntaxError   B) IndentationError   C) ExceptionError   D) ValueError

5. What does a Python package typically contain?
A) Only one module   B) A collection of modules
C) A single function   D) Only classes and methods

Long Answer Questions

1. Explain the process of reading from and writing to a text file in Python.

2. Describe the format operator in Python

3. How can command line arguments be handled in a Python program.

4. What are errors and exceptions in Python?

5. Discuss the concept of modules and packages in Python.

 **5.**

Object-Oriented Programming

Unit Structure

5.0 Classes and Objects

Class

In Python everything is an object. To create objects we required some Model or Plan or Blue print, which is nothing but class. We can write a class to represent properties (attributes) and actions (behavior) of object. Class represents the general or common characteristic of a group of objects.

- Properties can be represented by variables
- Actions can be represented by Methods or functions.
Hence class contains both variables and methods.

Define a class
We can define a class by using class keyword.

Syntax:

```
class className:
      variables:
      methods:
```

```
class Student:
     def xyz(self):
       print("xyz is executed")

s1=Student()
s1.xyz()
s1.xyz()
```

Output

```
xyz is executed
xyz is executed
```

Object

Object is an instance of a class. Physical existence of a class is nothing but object. We can create any number of objects for a class.

Syntax:

```
Object_name = classname()
```

Example:

```
s = Student()
```

5.1   Constructors and self variable

Constructor:

- Constructor is a special method in python.
- The name of the constructor should be __init__(self)
- Constructor will be executed automatically at the time of object creation.
- The main purpose of constructor is to declare and initialize instance variables.
- Per object constructor will be executed only once.
- Constructor can take at least one argument(atleast self)

```python
class Student:

    def __init__(self):
        print("Constructor is executed")

    def xyz(self):
        print("xyz is executed")

s1=Student()
s2=Student()

s1.xyz()
```

Output

```
Constructor is executed
Constructor is executed

xyz is executed
```

Self-variable:

self is the default variable which is always pointing to current object (like this keyword in Java) By using
self we can access instance variables and instance methods of object.

Note:
self should be first parameter inside constructor def __init__(self):

self should be first parameter inside instance methods def talk(self):

Example:

```python
def __init__(self,name,rollno,marks):
        self.name=name
        self.rollno=rollno
        self.marks=marks
```

```python
class Student:
    def __init__(self):
        self.name='Ajay'
        self.age=40
        self.marks=80

    def talk(self):
        print("Hello I am :",self.name)
        print("My Age is:",self.age)
        print("My Marks are:",self.marks)

s1=Student()
s1.talk()
```

Output

```
Hello I am : ajay
My Age is: 40
My Marks are: 80
```

Differences between Methods and Constructors:

Method	Constructor
1. Name of method can be any name	1. Constructor name should be always __init__
2. Method will be executed if we call that method	2. Constructor will be executed automatically at the time of object creation.
3. Per object, method can be called any number of times.	3. Per object, Constructor will be executed only once
4. Inside method we can write business logic	4. Inside Constructor we have to declare and initialize instance variables

Types of Variables:

1. Instance Variables (Object Level Variables)
2. Static Variables (Class Level Variables)
3. Local variables (Method Level Variables)

1. Instance Variable

If the value of a variable is varied from object to object, then such type of variables are called instance variables. For every object a separate copy of instance variables will be created.

Where we can declare Instance variables:

Inside Constructor by using self-variable:

We can declare instance variables inside a constructor by using self-keyword. Once we create object, automatically these variables will be added to the object.

Example:

```
class Employee:

    def __init__(self):
        self.eno=100
        self.ename='Ajay'
        self.esal=10000

e=Employee()
print(e.__dict__)
```

Output:

{'eno': 100, 'ename': 'Ajay', 'esal': 10000}

Accessing Instance variables:

We can access instance variables with in the class by using self-variable and outside of the class by using object reference.

Example:

```
class Test:
    def __init__(self):
        self.a=10
        self.b=20

    def display(self):
        print(self.a)
        print(self.b)

t=Test()
t.display()
print(t.a,t.b)
```

Output

```
10
20
10 20
```

2. Static variables

If the value of a variable is not varied from object to object, such type of variables we have to declare within the class directly but outside of methods. Such types of variables are called Static variables. For total class only one copy of static variable will be created and shared by all objects of that class. We can access static variables either by class name or by object reference.

Note: In the case of instance variables for every object a separate copy will be created, but in the case of static variables for total class only one copy will be created and shared by every object of that class.

```python
class Test:
    x=10

    def __init__(self):
        self.y=20

t1=Test()
t2=Test()

print('t1:',t1.x,t1.y)
print('t2:',t2.x,t2.y)

Test.x=888
t1.y=999

print('t1:',t1.x,t1.y)
print('t2:',t2.x,t2.y)
```

Output

```
t1: 10 20
t2: 10 20
t1: 888 999
t2: 888 20
```

3.Local variable

Sometimes to meet temporary requirements of programmer, we can declare variables inside a method directly, such type of variables are called local variable or temporary variables. Local variables will be created at the time of method execution and destroyed once method completes. Local variables of a method cannot be accessed from outside of method.

Example:

```python
class Test:
    def m1(self):
        a=1000
        print(a)

    def m2(self):
        b=2000
        print(b)
t=Test()
t.m1()
t.m2()
```

Output

```
1000
2000
```


5.2 Types of Methods

Types of Methods

Inside Python class 3 types of methods are allowed

1. Instance Methods
2. Class Methods
3. Static Methods

1. Instance Methods

Inside method implementation if we are using instance variables then such type of methods are called instance methods. Inside instance method declaration, we have to pass self variable.

def m1(self):

By using self variable inside method we can able to access instance variables. Within the class we can call instance method by using self variable and from outside of the class we can call by using object reference.

```python
class Student:

    def __init__(self,name,marks):
        self.name=name
        self.marks=marks

    def display(self):
        print('Hi',self.name)
        print('Your Marks are:',self.marks)

    def grade(self):
        if self.marks>=60:
            print('You got First Grade')
        elif self.marks>=50:
            print('Yout got Second Grade')
        elif self.marks>=35:
            print('You got Third Grade')
        else:
            print('You are Failed')
```

```python
n=int(input('Enter number of students:'))

for i in range(n):
    name=input('Enter Name:')
    marks=int(input('Enter Marks:'))

    s= Student(name,marks)
    s.display()
    s.grade()

print()
```

Output:

```
Enter number of students:2
Enter Name:abhi
Enter Marks:20
Hi abhi
Your Marks are: 20
You are Failed

Enter Name:akshay
Enter Marks:70
Hi akshay
Your Marks are: 70
You got First Grade
```

2. Class Methods

Inside method implementation if we are using only class variables (static variables), then such type of methods we should declare as class method. We can declare class method explicitly by using @classmethod decorator.

For class method we should provide cls variable at the time of declaration We can call classmethod by using classname or object reference variable.

Program

```python
class Animal:
    legs=4

    @classmethod
    def walk(cls,name):
        print('{} walks with {} legs...'.format(name,cls.legs))

Animal.walk('Dog')
Animal.walk('Cat')
```

Output

```
Dog walks with 4 legs...
Cat walks with 4 legs...
```

3. Static Method

In general these methods are general utility methods. Inside these methods we won't use any instance or class variables. Here we won't provide self or cls arguments at the time of declaration.

We can declare static method explicitly by using @staticmethod decorator. We can access static methods by using classname or object reference

```python
class DemoMath:

    @staticmethod
    def add(x,y):
        print('The Sum:',x+y)

    @staticmethod
    def product(x,y):
        print('The Product:',x*y)

    @staticmethod
    def average(x,y):
        print('The average:',(x+y)/2)

DemoMath.add(10,20)
DemoMath.product(10,20)
DemoMath.average(10,20)
```

Output

```
The Sum: 30
The Product: 200
The average: 15.0
```

Note: In general, we can use only instance and static methods. Inside static method we can access class level variables by using class name. class methods are most rarely used methods in python.

Inner classes

Sometimes we can declare a class inside another class, such type of classes are called inner classes. Without existing one type of object if there is no chance of existing another type of object, then we should go for inner classes.

Example: Without existing university object there is no chance of existing Department object

```
class University:
     .....
        class Department:
           ......
```

Program:

```
class Outer:
   def __init__(self):
      print("outer class object creation")

   class Inner:
      def __init__(self):
         print("inner class object creation")

      def m1(self):
         print("inner class method")

o=Outer()
i=o.Inner()
i.m1()
```

Output

```
outer class object creation
inner class object creation
inner class method
```

Destructors:

Destructor is a special method and the name should be __del__ .Just before destroying an object Garbage Collector always calls destructor to perform clean up activities (Resource deallocation activities like close database connection etc). Once destructor execution completed then Garbage Collector automatically destroys that object.

Note: The job of destructor is not to destroy object and it is just to perform clean up activities.

Example:

```
class Test:

    def __init__(self):
        print("Object Initialization...")

    def __del__(self):
        print("performing clean up activities...")

t1=Test()

t1=None

print("End of application")
```

Output

```
Object Initialization...
performing clean up activities...
End of application
```

5.4 Inheritance.

Inheritance

Inheritance is a way of creating new class for using the details of existing class without modifying it. Inheritance allows us to define a class that inherits all the methods and properties from another class. The process of creating new classes from existing class is called as inheritance.
The new classes are called as the subclasses or derived classes or child class, while existing class is called as base class or parent class

Syntax

```
class parentclass:
        Statement

class childclass(parentclass):
        Statement
```

Types of Inheritance

Depending upon the pattern in which the base class and its derived classes are arranged, there are different types of inheritance as follows:

1)Single Inheritance
2)Multilevel Inheritance
3) Hierarchical Inheritance
4)Multiple Inheritance
5)Hybrid Inheritance

1. Single Inheritance:

The concept of inheriting the properties from one class to another class is known as single inheritance.

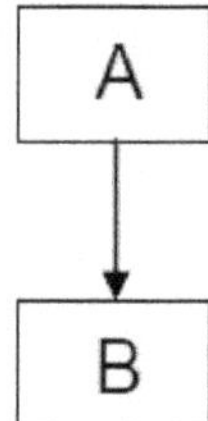

Eg:

```
class P:
    def m1(self):
        print("Parent Method")

class C(P):
    def m2(self):
        print("Child Method")

c=C()
c.m1()
c.m2()
```

Output:

```
Parent Method
Child Method
```

2. Multi-Level Inheritance:

In multilevel inheritance, a class is derived from another sub class that is the sub class is acting as a base class for deriving new classes.

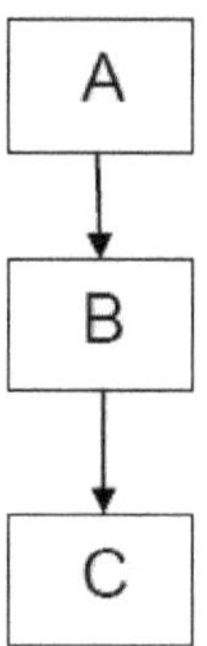

Example:

```
class P:
    def m1(self):
        print("Parent Method")

class C(P):
    def m2(self):
        print("Child Method")
class CC(C):
    def m3(self):
        print("Sub Child Method")

c=CC()
c.m1()
c.m2()
c.m3()
```

Output:

```
Parent Method
Child Method
Sub Child Method
```

3. Hierarchical Inheritance:

The concept of inheriting properties from one class into multiple classes which are present at same level is known as Hierarchical Inheritance

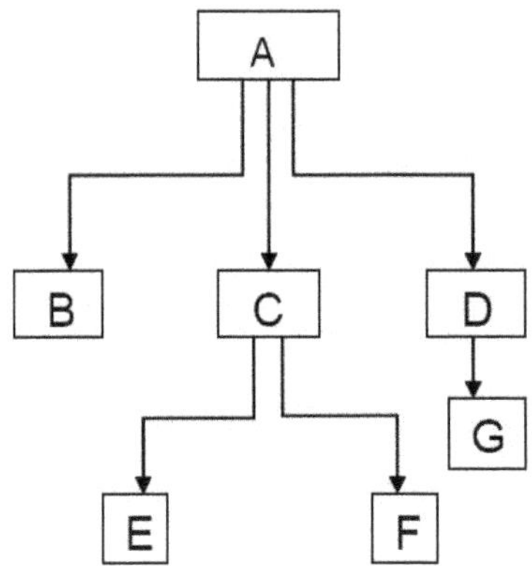

```
class P:
    def m1(self):
        print("Parent Method")

class C1(P):
    def m2(self):
        print("Child1 Method")

class C2(P):
    def m3(self):
        print("Child2 Method")

c1=C1()
c1.m1()
c1.m2()

c2=C2()
c2.m1()
c2.m3()
```

Output:

```
Parent Method
Child1 Method
Parent Method
Child2 Method
```

4. Multiple Inheritance:

The concept of inheriting the properties from multiple classes into a single class at a time, is known as multiple inheritance.

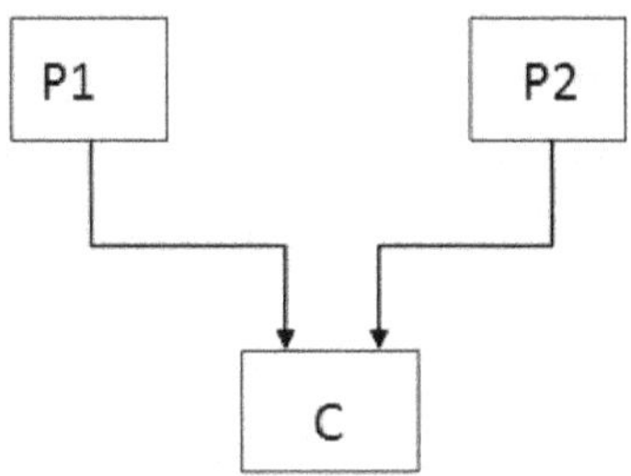


```
class P1:
    def m1(self):
        print("Parent1 Method")

class P2:
    def m2(self):
        print("Parent2 Method")

class C(P1,P2):
    def m3(self):
        print("Child2 Method")

c=C()

c.m1()
c.m2()
c.m3()
```

Output:

```
Parent1 Method
Parent2 Method
Child2 Method
```

5.Hybrid Inheritance:

Combination of Single, Multilevel, multiple and Hierarchical inheritance is known as Hybrid Inheritance.

Program

```
class A:
    def show(self):
        print('show function from class A')
```

```python
class B(A):
    def display(self):
        print('display function from B')

class D:
    def output(self):
        print('output function from class D')

class C(B,D):
    def prints(self):
        print('print function form sub class')

obj1=A()
obj1.show()

obj2=B()
obj2.show()
obj2.display()

obj3=D()
obj3.output()

obj4=C()
obj4.show()
obj4.display()
obj4.output()
obj4.prints()
```

Output

```
show function from class A
show function from class A
display function from B
output function from class D
show function from class A
display function from B
output function from class D
print function form sub class
```

super () Method

super () is a built-in method which is useful to call the super class constructors, variables and methods from the child class. In method overriding, the subclass method is defined with the same name as that of the method in the base class.

When the method is called through the subclass object, it will execute the subclass method, but even if the base class method is overriding in the subclass but still it is required to call the base class method then the super keyword is to be used.

Program:

```python
class abc:
    def show(self):
    print('show method is executed from base class')

class xyz(abc):
  def show(self):
    print('show method is executed from sub class')

  def display(self):
    super().show()
    self.show()
    print('display method is executed from sub class')

s1=xyz()
s1.display()
```

Output

```
show method is executed from base class
show method is executed from sub class
display method is executed from sub class
```

5.5 Polymorphism.

Polymorphism

Poly means many. Morphs means forms.
Polymorphism means 'Many Forms'.

Eg1: Yourself is best example of polymorphism. In front of your parents You will have one type of behaviour and with friends another type of behaviour. Same person but different behaviours at different places, which is nothing but polymorphism.

Overloading

We can use same operator or methods for different purposes.

Eg1: + operator can be used for Arithmetic addition and String concatenation

```python
print(10+20)#30
print('soft'+'ware')#software
```

Eg2: * operator can be used for multiplication and string repetition purposes.

print(10*20)#200
print('hello'*3)#hellohellohello

There are 3 types of overloading

1. Method Overloading
2. Constructor Overloading
3. Operator Overloading

1. Method Overloading:

If two methods having same name but different type of arguments then those methods are said to be overloaded methods.

Example:

m1(int a)
m1(double d)

But in Python Method overloading is not possible.

If we are trying to declare multiple methods with same name and different number of arguments then Python will always consider only last method.

Demo Program:

```
class Test:

    def m1(self):
        print('no arg method')

    def m1(self,a):
        print('one arg method')

    def m1(self,a,b):
        print('two arg method')

t=Test()
t.m1()  #Error
t.m1(10) #Error
t.m1(10,20)
```

Output

```
TypeError: m1() missing 2 required positional arguments: 'a' and 'b'
```

In the above program python will consider only last method.

How can we handle overloaded method requirements in Python?

Most of the times, if method with variable number of arguments required then we can handle with default arguments or with variable number of argument methods.

Demo Program with Default Arguments:

```python
class Test:

    def sum(self,a=None,b=None,c=None):

        if a!=None and b!= None and c!= None:
            print('The Sum of 3 Numbers:',a+b+c)
        elif a!=None and b!= None:
            print('The Sum of 2 Numbers:',a+b)
        elif a!=None:
            print('The Square=:',a*a)
        else:
            print('You have not passed any argument')

t=Test()
t.sum(10,20)
t.sum(10,20,30)
t.sum(10)
t.sum()
```

Output

```
The Sum of 2 Numbers: 30
The Sum of 3 Numbers: 60
The Square=: 100
You have not passed any argument
```

2. Constructor Overloading:

Constructor overloading is not possible in Python. If we define multiple constructors then the last constructor will be considered.

```python
class Test:
    def __init__(self):
        print('No arg Constructor')

    def __init__(self,a):
        print('One arg constructor')
```

```python
    def __init__(self,a,b):
        print('Two arg constructor')

#t1=Test() Error
#t1=Test(10)Error
t1=Test(10,20)
```

In the above program only we get the output for last constructor

Output:

```
Two arg Constructor
```

But based on our requirement we can declare constructor with default arguments and variable number of arguments.

Operator Overloading

We can use the same operator for multiple purposes, which is nothing but operator overloading.

Python supports operator overloading.

Eg1: + operator can be used for Arithmetic addition and String concatenation

Program to use + operator for our class objects:

```python
class Book:
    def __init__(self,pages):
        self.pages=pages

b1=Book(100)
b2=Book(200)
print(b1+b2)
```

Output

```
TypeError: unsupported operand type(s) for +: 'Book' and 'Book'
```

We can overload + operator to work with Book objects also

For every operator Magic Methods are available. To overload any operator, we have to override that Method in our class.

Internally + operator is implemented by using __add__ () method. This method is called magic method for + operator. We must override this method in our class.

Program to overload + operator for our Book class objects:

```python
class Book:
    def __init__(self,pages):
        self.pages=pages

    def __add__(self,z):
        t=self.pages+z.pages
        return t

b1=Book(100)
b2=Book(200)

x=b1+b2
print('The Total Number of Pages:',x)
```

Output

```
The Total Number of Pages: 300
```

The following is the list of operators and corresponding magic methods.

+	__add__()	/=	__idiv__()
-	__sub__()	//=	__ifloordiv__()
*	__mul__()	%=	__imod__()
/	__div__()	**=	__ipow__()
//	__floordiv__()	<	__lt__()
%	__mod__()	<=	__le__()
**	__pow__()	>	__gt__()
+=	__iadd__()	>=	__ge__()
-=	__isub__()	==	__eq__()
*=	__imul__()	!=	__ne__()

5.6 Functional Programming.

In functional programming, a program consists entirely of evaluation of pure functions. It has two abilities

1. To take another function as an argument
2. To return another function to its caller

```
def func():
        print("I am function func()!")

func()
x=func
x()
```

The assignment x = func creates a new reference to func() named x. You can pass a function to another function as an argument:

```
def inner():
   print("I am function inner()!")
def outer(inner):
   inner()
outer(inner)
```

output
```
I am function inner()!
```

The call passes inner() as an argument to outer(). Within outer(), Python binds inner() to the function parameter function. outer() can then call inner() directly via function. This is known as function composition.

Python provides a shortcut notation called a decorator to facilitate wrapping one function inside another. When you pass a function to another function, the passed-in function sometimes is referred to as a callback because a call back to the inner function can modify the outer function's behavior.

Defining an Anonymous Function With lambda

Functional programming is all about calling functions and passing them around. You can always define a function in the usual way, using the def keyword.

The syntax of a lambda expression is as follows:

```
lambda <parameter_list>: <expression>
```

lambda   keyword

<parameter_list>   comma-separated list of parameter names

<expression>   An expression usually involving the names in <parameter_list>

The value of a lambda expression is a callable function, just like a function defined with the def keyword. It takes arguments, as specified by <parameter_list>, and returns a value, as indicated by <expression>.

```
reverse = lambda s: s[::-1]

x=reverse("I am a string")

print(x)
```

```
arth=(lambda x1, x2, x3: (x1 + x2 + x3) / 3)
b=arth(9, 6, 6)
print(b)
```

output

7.0

Applying a Function to an Iterable With map()

map() is a Python built-in function. With map(), you can apply a function to each element in an iterable in turn, and map() will return an iterator that yields the results.

The syntax for calling map() on a single iterable looks like this:

map(<f>, <iterable>)

```
def reverse(s):
    return s[::-1]
animals = ["cat", "dog", "cow", "goat"]
iterator = map(reverse, animals)
for i in iterator:
    print(i)
```

output

```
tac
god
woc
taog
```

```
animals = ["cat", "dog", "cow", "goat"]
iterator = map(lambda s: s[::-1], animals)
print(list(iterator))
```

calling map () With Multiple Iterables

There's another form of map () that takes more than one iterable argument:

map(<f>, <iterable₁>, <iterable₂>, ..., <iterableₙ>)

```
def f(a, b, c):
        return a + b + c
print(list(map(f, [1, 2, 3], [10, 20, 30], [100, 200, 300])))
```

In this case, f () takes three arguments. Correspondingly, there are three iterable arguments to map (): the lists [1, 2, 3], [10, 20, 30], and [100, 200, 300].

The first item returned is the result of applying f() to the first element in each list: f(1, 10, 100). The second item returned is f(2, 20, 200), and the third is f(3, 30, 300), as shown in the following diagram:

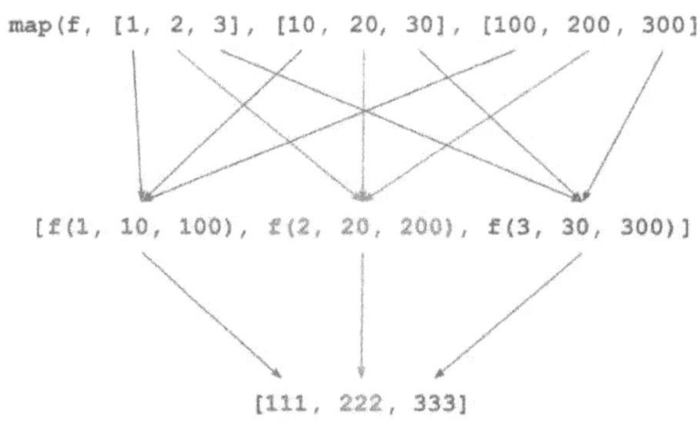

filter () allows you to select or filter items from an iterable .

filter(<f>, <iterable>)

filter(<f>, <iterable>) applies function <f> to each element of <iterable> and returns an iterator that yields all items for which <f> is truthy. Conversely, it filters out all items for which <f> is falsy.

select only the even numbers from the list and filter out the odd numbers:

```python
def is_even(x):
        return x % 2 == 0
print(list(filter(is_even, range(10))))
```

```python
print(list(filter(lambda x: x % 2 == 0, range(10))))
```

output

```
    [0, 2, 4, 6, 8]
```

reduce()

reduce() applies a function to the items in an iterable two at a time, progressively combining them to produce a single result.

```python
from functools import reduce
def f(x, y):
    return x + y
print(reduce(f, [1, 2, 3, 4, 5]))
```

This call to reduce() produces the result 15 from the list [1, 2, 3, 4, 5] as follows:

```
                    1 + 2
    f(1, 2) = 3
            ↓       3 + 3
        f(3, 3) = 6
                ↓       6 + 4
            f(6, 4) = 10
                    ↓       10 + 5
                f(10, 5) = 15

            reduce(f, [1, 2, 3, 4, 5])
```

```python
from functools import reduce
def f(x, y):
    return x * y

print(reduce(f, [120]))
print(reduce(f,[4,5,7,3,2,6,8]))
```

Python Generators

In Python, a generator is a function that returns an iterator that produces a sequence of values when iterated over. Generators are useful when we want to produce a large sequence of values, but we don't want to store all of them in memory at once.

we can define a generator function using the def keyword, but instead of the return statement we use the yield statement.

```
def generator_name(arg):
    # statements
    yield something
```

Here, the yield keyword is used to produce a value from the generator. When the generator function is called, it does not execute the function body immediately. Instead, it returns a generator object that can be iterated over to produce the values. Here's an example of a generator function that produces a sequence of numbers,

```
def my_generator(n):
    value = 0

    while value < n:
        yield value
        value += 1

for value in my_generator(3):
    print(value)
```

output

```
0
1
2
```

In the above example, the my_generator() generator function takes an integer n as an argument and produces a sequence of numbers from 0 to n-1.

The yield keyword is used to produce a value from the generator and pause the generator function's execution until the next value is requested.The for loop iterates over the generator object produced by my_generator(), and the print statement prints each value produced by the generator.

```python
def my_generator(n):
    value = 0


    while value < n:
        yield value
        value += 1

generator = my_generator(3)
print(next(generator))  # 0
print(next(generator))  # 1
print(next(generator))  # 2
```

Python Generator Expression

In Python, a generator expression is a concise way to create a generator object.

syntax,

        (expression for item in iterable)

Here, expression is a value that will be returned for each item in the iterable.

```python
# create the generator object
squares_generator = (i * i for i in range(5))

for i in squares_generator:
        print(i)
```

Output

```
0
1
4
9
16
```

5.7 Summary.

In Python, classes and objects are fundamental concepts in object-oriented programming. A class serves as a blueprint for creating objects, encapsulating data attributes (variables) and methods (functions) that operate on the data. Objects are instances of a class, created using a constructor method, typically defined as __init__().

Multiple objects can be created from a single class, each with its own set of attributes. Class attributes are shared across all instances, whereas instance (or data) attributes are specific to each object. Inheritance allows a class (child) to inherit attributes and methods from another class (parent), promoting code

reusability. Polymorphism enables methods to perform different tasks based on the object that calls them, enhancing flexibility and integration in code design.

Functional programming in Python emphasizes the use of functions to process data. Lambda functions are small, anonymous functions defined with the lambda keyword, useful for short, throwaway functions. Iterators and generators are constructs that allow for lazy evaluation of data sequences. An iterator is an object with a __next__() method, which retrieves items one at a time. Generators, defined with the yield keyword, produce iterators and allow functions to return an iterable set of items, one at a time, conserving memory and enabling efficient looping through large datasets.

5.8 Questions.

Multiple Choice Questions

1. What is the primary purpose of the init method in a Python class?

a) To define a class attribute   b) To initialize instance attributes
c) To create class methods   d) To delete an object

2. Which of the following is true about class attributes and instance attributes in Python?

a) Class attributes are unique to each object, while instance attributes are shared among all instances.
b) Class attributes are defined within methods, while instance attributes are defined outside of methods.
c) Class attributes are shared among all instances of the class, while instance attributes are unique to each object.
d) Class attributes can only be accessed within the class, while instance attributes can be accessed from outside the class.

3. What is encapsulation in object-oriented programming?

a) A technique to reduce the size of objects
b) A method for defining multiple classes
c) A mechanism to restrict direct access to some of an object's components
d) A way to inherit methods and properties from another class

4. Which of the following is an example of a lambda function in Python?

a) def lambda(x): return x * 2   b) lambda x: x * 2
c) lambda(x) { return x * 2 }   d) function(x) -> x * 2

5.What is the main advantage of using generators in Python?
a) They allow for defining anonymous functions.
b) They enable immediate execution of a sequence of statements.
c) They produce items one at a time and conserve memory.
d) They simplify the inheritance process.

Long Answer Questions

1. Explain the concept of object-oriented programming in Python with an emphasis on classes and objects.

2. Describe the differences between class attributes and instance attributes in Python. How are they defined and accessed?

3.What is encapsulation in object-oriented programming, and why is it important?

4. Discuss the principles of inheritance and polymorphism in Python.

Glossary

A

- Argument
- Array
- Assignment

B

- Boolean
- Break

C

- Class
- Concatenation
- Conditional

D

- Dictionary
- Debugging
- Decorator

E

- Exception
- Else
- Expression

F

- Function
- For Loop
- Float

G

- Generator
- Global Variable

H

- Hashing

I

- Indentation
- Iterable
- Import

R

- Range
- Recursion
- Return

S

- Set
- Slice
- String
- Syntax

T

- Tuple
- Type

U

- Unicode
- Unpacking

V

- Variable
- Virtual Environment

W

- While Loop
- With Statement

Y

- Yield

Z

- ZeroDivisionError